Catalinas and Su
on
Lough Erne, Ireland
in
World War Two

The Aftermath
of the Donegal Corridor

To Felix with best wishes from Joe 2nd April 2013

By Joe O'Loughlin

Copyright ©Joe O'Loughlin, 2013

First Published in Ireland, in 2013, in co-operation with
Choice Publishing, Drogheda, County Louth, Republic of Ireland
www.choicepublishing.ie

ISBN: 978-1-909154-19-3

All rights reserved. No part of this publication may be reproduced, stored in a retrieval system, transmitted in any form, or by any means, electronic, mechanical, photocopying, recording or otherwise, without the prior permission of the copyright holder.

Catalinas and Sunderlands on Lough Erne, Ireland in World War Two

The Aftermath of the Donegal Corridor

Dedicated to the late Brian Pendry, Chairman of the Fermanagh Flying Boat Association

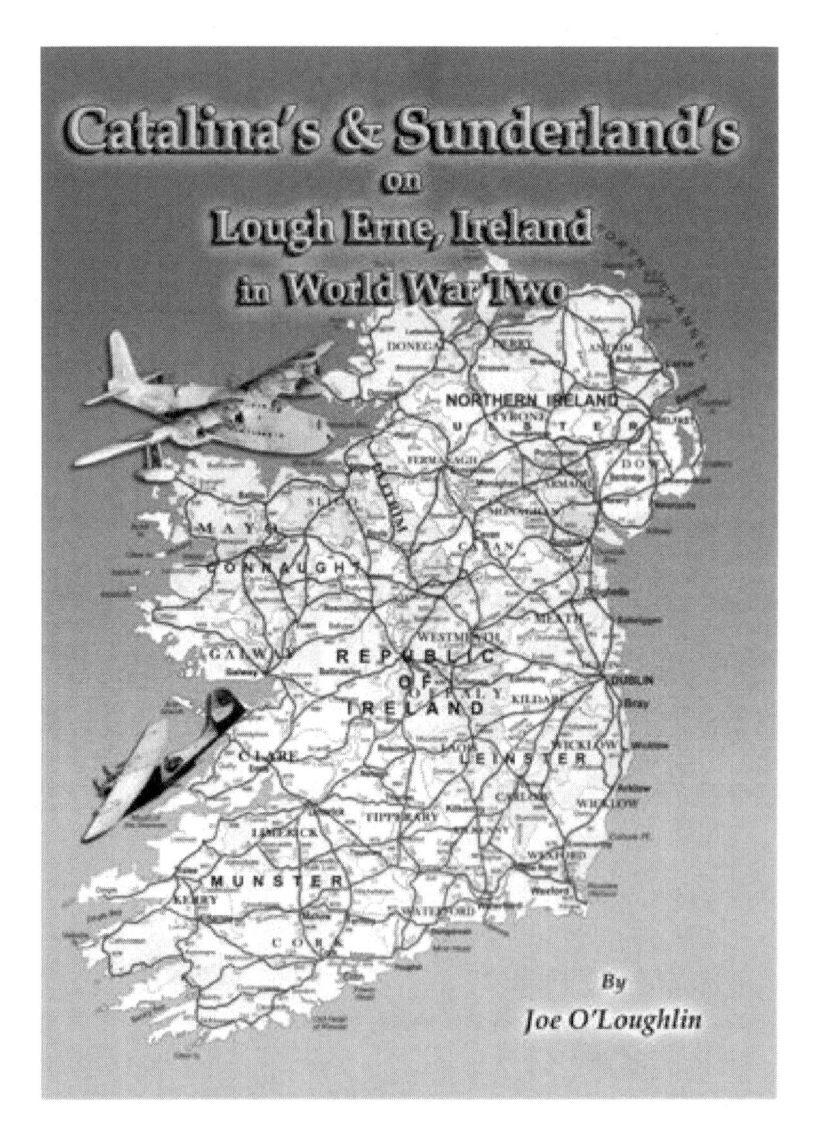

Map of Ireland with pictures of a Catalina and Sunderland

CONTENTS

Introduction
Acknowledgements
Preface
Chapter 1   Catalina AM266 1
Chapter 2   Why Did Nana Cry Sunderland DW 110.................... 9
Chapter 3   A True Story of Sunderland NJ 175 23
Chapter 4   Sunderland W3988 – Doonbeg, Co. Clare 32
Chapter 5   Sunderland W4036 and the Dolphin Family 47
Chapter 6   Norm Muffitt and the Fate of Catalina FP 120 55
Chapter 7   Ground crews at Castle Archdale 66
Chapter 8   A New Zealander returns to Castle Archdale 74
Photo Gallery... 84
Chapter 9   An ex-RAF Officer visits Lough Erne 103
Chapter 10   Relatives of crew members get history of crashes 111
Chapter 11   Crashes at Lough Erne, the Donegal Corridor and
                 Neutral Ireland.. 121
Chapter 12   Lost at Sea – They Have No Known Graves 133
Chapter 13   Short Bursts – A Canadian Journal 138
Chapter 14   A Selection of Stories and Events 145
Chapter 15   Crash Memorials and Letters of Appreciation 155
Chapter 16   The Ports and Irish Neutrality 173
Chapter 17   Kathleen Winters – Aviation Author with Roots
                 in Donegal 180
Conclusion 184

INTRODUCTION

Since the publication of my book "Voices of the Donegal Corridor" in 2005, and the setting up of my website (www.joeoloughlin.co.uk) in July 2008, much new information has come to hand about some of the other 200 World War 2 plane crashes in neutral Ireland and several that happened off the west coast of Ireland, some of them near Donegal. There were a number of crashes here in Co. Fermanagh and throughout Northern Ireland. More important still is the number of families of those who lost their lives; who have come here to Irvinestown, Co. Fermanagh, to visit war graves, where they exist, and crash sites, where possible, in Donegal and other parts of Ireland. Breege McCusker, Gary Pentland and I have met with many of the families and provided them with information that they did not have. Naturally this was a great comfort to next of kin, as all they had was the brief inadequate official telegram notifying them that a father, son, brother or husband had died in action.

Here in the island of Ireland there are a number of people who have a deep interest in WW2 aviation, individually these people have accumulated a vast amount of information. They are not selfish people, as some times historians can be. They have shared the results of their research with people like me. Their reward is to be found in the comfort and closure that the information has brought to so many families not only in Ireland, but in Great Britain, the U.S.A., Canada, Australia, New Zealand, Poland, and even Germany.

In the years of conflict during the Second World War, as in all other wars, families who had young men serving in the forces dreaded the knock on the door and the delivery of a telegram telling that a husband, father or son had been lost in action. In some cases a Chaplain or commanding officer would send a letter of sympathy giving brief details of the incident that resulted in the death of a loved one.

The details of the many Irish crashes are available on the web site www.skynet.ie/~dan/war/crashes.htm created by Dennis Burke of Tubbercurry, County Sligo. It includes the names of those who died and those who survived. This is one of the most valuable sources of information on that period of Irish history. Other people who, along with Dennis, have valuable information on the period, and who have willingly shared it with me, are Tony Kearns in Dublin, Anne Tierney in Tuam, Co. Galway, Breege McCusker in Irvinestown, County Fermanagh, Martin Gleeson, Gary Pentland, Gortin, Jimmy McLaughlin, Les Ingram, and James Stewart, in Omagh, Co Tyrone.

ACKNOWLEDGEMENTS

It just would not be possible to produce a book like this one without the help and support and encouragement of a great number of people. The most important source of valuable information is with out doubt the detailed website compiled by Dennis Burke, without it, this journal could not have been produced. I had hoped at one time that Dennis, and that other great authority, on the period, Tony Kearns, of Dublin, might have written books containing the vast amount of knowledge they have, but so far that has not been possible. Therefore it has fallen my lot to write this book. I do have several advantages, in the fact that I lived through the Wold War 2 years and I was on occasions an eye witness to some important events. Living here in Co. Fermanagh and since I retired in 1997, I have had the time to work on the project. The following is a list of the people who have helped me. I may have forgotten some names, and hopefully like any author, I will be pardoned for such errors. There are others who wish to remain anonymous and I respect their wishes. They know who they are.

Dennis Burke: Sinéad Fox; Katie Frazer; Martin Gleeson; Les and Maureen Ingram; Tony Kearns; Breege McCusker; James McLaughlin; Marian O'Keeffe; Richard O'Loughlin; Gary Pentland; James Stewart; Anne Tierney; and Dyan Tucker. Ballyshannon Town Council; Donegal County Council; Fermanagh District Council; and the Irish Military Archives, Cathal Brugha Barracks, Dublin.

Two most important functions in the production of a book; are the graphic design, and the proof reading of the manuscript. My cousin, Sinéad Fox, who is a fully qualified graphic designer, has done an excellent job and I am grateful to her for the finished product. The choice of my good friend and fellow members of the Clogher Historical Society, Marian O'Keeffe, has proved to be an excellent one.

Marian has been most meticulous in finding the many corrections that had to be made, before finally going to print. For the work of both ladies I am extremely thankful.

My thanks, also to my wife; Ina, who took so many phone calls and messages in connection with the book. Also to our son Richard, who kept the computer in order when it gave problems.

There are two people who have done great research into the crash of Sunderland DW110 on the Blue Stack Mountains, in Co. Donegal. They are Dennis Burke, Tubbercorry, Co. Sligo, and Dyan Tucker, now living in New Zealand. Her cousin, Maurice Vincent Wareing died in that crash. Her website is www.freewebs.com/DW110. The website of the Irish Military Archives, Cathal Brugha Barracks, Dublin is www.militaryarchives.ie They have been more that helpful in supplying reports on the crashes. The website of Dennis Burke is given elsewhere in this book. Without the help of such people it would not be possible to compile a history of World War two in Ireland.

PREFACE

What was the Donegal Corridor?

Some history of the island of Ireland is required to explain the Donegal Corridor. For centuries Ireland had been ruled by England. From 1916 a fight for independence from English rule took place until 1921, when twenty six of the thirty two counties were granted independence. This part of Ireland became known as Eire or The Irish Free State. The six counties of the North East choose to remain part of the U.K and became known as Northern Ireland. In the mid 1930's there were strong rumours of war breaking out in Europe. The Irish government declared a policy of neutrality. Being a young nation in its own right for just 15 years, Eire was still suffering from the fight for independence and a bitter civil war that followed it. She was in no position to become involved in a conflict between the major nations of the world.

The policy of neutrality taken by the deValera government was fully supported by all elected political parties. The longest battle of World War 2 – the Battle of the Atlantic - commenced after the war started in September 1939, and continued until May 1945, when the war ended. German U-boats and air craft attacked Allied shipping convoys sinking hundreds of ships and large quantities of supplies coming from Canada and the U.S.A. to Britain. Thousands of lives were lost including those of refugees going to Canada.

In late December 1940, Lough Erne in Northern Ireland was surveyed to see if it was suitable for a flying boat base that could be put to immediate use. This was the most westerly point in the U.K. from where planes could patrol the Atlantic and offer some protection to the shipping convoys against the dreaded U-boats. Early in 1941, the first Flying Boats were based on Lough Erne. As they were not permitted to fly over the neutral territory of the Irish Free State, they had to fly north and around the coast of Co. Donegal. The distance they could travel was thus restricted. Aircraft from Canada were also restricted by how far they could patrol. This left a large space of the Atlantic where there was no air cover, and this became known as 'The Black Gap', where the U-boats could operate freely.

In January 1941, a meeting took place between Taoiseach Eamon deValera, (The Irish Prime Minister), and Sir John Maffey, the British representative in Dublin. An agreement was reached whereby the Lough Erne based flying boats were permitted to fly across a four mile stretch of neutral Eire, from Belleek in Co. Fermanagh to Ballyshannon in Co. Donegal. This stretch became know as the 'Donegal Corridor', and the flying boats could extend their patrols westward by at least 100 miles. To pacify the Germans, the aircraft were supposed to follow a defined route and then were only to partake in air/sea rescue missions. At official level this agreement was top secret, and was only made public after the war was over. To those of us who lived locally it was no secret, as we watched the planes fly overhead every day. The original rules were soon adapted to suit the occasion, and Lough Erne based planes went on patrol, not only out over the Atlantic, and also out over the North Sea, and south over the Bay of Biscay as far as Gibraltar. This was a turning point in the Battle of the Atlantic, as the Sunderland and Catalina planes sank at least 9 U-boats, and damaged many more that had to return to base in Brest, France.

There is no doubt that Hitler was fully aware of this concession, as I often heard Lord Haw-Haw (William Joyce) broadcasting on 'Germany Calling', refer to 'The Swans on Lough Erne' as he called the flying boats. The use of the Donegal Corridor more than made up for the loss to Britain of the shipping ports in Eire, as at the time England was not in a position to man or equip them. Also, the ports were within easy range of the German bombers and U-boats based in occupied France. The days of the large battle ships being important in modern warfare were coming to a close, as many of them on either side were sunk in the early stages the war.

One of the most famous Atlantic patrols was that of the Catalina AH545 of 209 Squadron, R.A.F., which spotted the Bismarck when it was escaping to France. Over 40 aircraft were lost, and some 350 airmen lost their lives, while serving on Lough Erne. Much more could be written; instead, this short preface gives an insight to the importance of the Donegal Corridor. In April 2007, a plaque was unveiled on Belleek Bridge, and another on Ballyshannon Bridge, to commemorate the Donegal Corridor.

CHAPTER 1

Catalina AM 265.

The crash of Consolidated Catalina AM 265 at Aunagh Hill, Glenade, Co. Leitrim on 21st March 1941 and other crashes.

This aircraft was attached to 240 Squadron based at Castle Archdale, Lough Erne, Co. Fermanagh, Northern Ireland. The Catalina was tasked with searching the Atlantic for German U-boats. Such missions were regularly of up to 21 hours duration.

At 07:32 on the morning of 21St March 1941, Catalina AM 265 took off from Castle Archdale. It took off westerly heading towards the Atlantic. At 07:48, it was observed flying over Lough Erne again, as if it had encountered some problem. No distress call was heard from the Air Craft, and it re-established its course towards the coast. It was customary for the A/C on missions such as this to maintain Radio Silence unless in distress. At 08:05 it passed over Ballyshannon, where it turned south-west in the direction of Kinlough, where it passed over the village at 08:11. Minutes later it crashed into a mountain south of Kinlough at a height of 1,700 feet above sea level. It impacted with Aunagh Hill, Cloontypruglish on the Glenade side of Kinlough. All eight crew were killed instantly.

The local Defence Force (LDF) at Kinlough were contacted. They informed the military Barracks at Manorhamilton, who in turn reported the crash at 09:20 to army Intelligence (G2) at Athlone, Co. Westmeath. Captain Power, along with an attachment from Finner Camp located between Bundoran and Ballyshannon, Co. Donegal, arrived at the crash site at 13:30. The aircraft had burst into flames on impact, its full fuel load would have rendered the aircraft a smouldering wreck very soon. The aircraft was also carrying a quantity of depth charges, destined for any enemy U-boats it might encounter.

Under Pilot Officer Hisneker-Heaton, the British Military personnel arrived at the scene and were advised to contact Sir John Maffey, the U.K Representative in Eire. The crash site was cordoned off by the Irish Military from Finner Camp. The bodies of the crew were first laid out in a nearby cow byre. From there, they were carried on stretchers by members of the LDF down the rugged mountain side to the parish hall in Kinlough. On viewing the remains of one of the air crew, P/O Heaton was so disturbed that he ordered the remaining coffins to remain on-opened.

The above account of the last flight of Catalina AM265 was given to me by the late Frank Garvin of Belleek, former Flight Sergeant of the R.A.F. Others who contributed valuable information on the crash were Seamus Gormley, Dennis Burke and Mark Sheldon. Mark and his family have researched World War Two crash sites all over the British Isles including Ireland. With his friends Nick Wotherspoon and Alan Clark, he has co-authored a book *"Aircraft Wrecks" The walkers guide to historic crash sites on the Moors and mountains of the British Isles. (Including Ireland)* Mark supplied me with excellent photos of the crash site of AM 265, and of the inscribed memorial plaque erected there by Seamus Gormley of Whitehill, Roy Gibson, Jimmy Stephenson and Gary Pentland. The memorial was placed on land which is owned by the Meehan family of Glenade, who kindly gave their approval for its erection. As with the memorial on the Blue Stacks, all the materials including water had to be carried up the mountain side by hand.

In Memory of the air crew of Catalina AM 265 of 240 Squadron R.A.F. who were killed on this site on Friday 21st March 1941.

F/O Albert E. Whitworth; AC1 Ronald Oldfield; P/O Charles P. Davidson, (RCAF) age 27; Sgt. Gordon H. Slack age 21; Sgt. Henry Dunbar age 20; Sgt. Frederick R.A. Chalk age 25; F/O Harold L. Seward; and Sgt. Harry H. Newbury age 20. R.I.P.

Erected by Lough Erne Aviation Museum 1988.

On 21st November 2011, Julian Fowler the B.B.C. reporter for Co Fermanagh contacted me. He had received a request from Harry Dodd, whose uncle Sgt. Henry Dunbar was killed in the crash of Catalina AM 265. He only had sketchy details of the crash and naturally wished to have more information. Some years earlier Harry had, with his mother, who was a sister of Henry Dunbar, visited his grave in the Church of Ireland cemetery in

Irvinestown. Thankfully I was able to supply Harry with the full history of the crash, and photographs of the site and memorial plaque. Over the years since the publication of the book "Fermanagh and Castle Archdale in World War Two" by Breege McCusker, and my book "Voices of the Donegal Corridor", a number of families who lost relations in crashes contacted us for information. It has been a great comfort and form of closure to these families to learn the true facts of how their loved ones died. Little did the people who erected memorials on the sites realise how important their work would be many years later.

Sunderland W 3977

Sunderland W 3977 of 201 Squadron, Castle Archdale, took off from Lough Erne at 15:43 on Thursday 5th February, 1942. It was homeward bound on 6th February when it went missing. The Irish Coast Watching Service lookout post on the west coast of Donegal at Rossan Point Malin Bay, recorded hearing an explosion at sea in the early hours of the morning of 6th February. This was the only reliable information regarding the loss of the homeward bound Sunderland. Sometime later, wreckage was washed ashore but sadly no bodies were recovered. The families of the crew were notified that the men were missing in action when their aircraft failed to return from a mission.

The Crew names are:- F/Lt. Francis Wilfred Smith; P/O. John Percival Bartlett; F/O Rodney Wyben Smith, RAAF; F/O Henry Kitchin; F/Sgt. Harold S. Mason; F/Sgt. Norman Clare; F/Sgt. John Frederick Charles Smith; Sgt. Arnold Alfred Rolfe; Sgt. Hugh Jones; Sgt. Kenneth C. Nutt; Sgt. Gordon W.E. Jacobson; and AC1 Eric Hopkinson.

An early enquiry from a relation of one of the crew was made to the late George Smith, who lived in Jersey Island. His story is recorded in another section of this journal. A remarkable thing about this aircraft is that there were three men named Smith on the crew, and that the enquiry came to a person also of the same name. George in turn referred the person to me. On 3rd May 2006, I had an e-mail from a Danielle Hurley, nee Smith, who lived in New South Wales Australia, looking for information about her Great Uncle Rodney. She had just found a file relating to Rodney. In the file was a telegram telling his parents that he was missing in action. There was also a letter from a Miss B. Challand, requesting his most current address, and a reply letter telling her that he was missing in action. She must have been his girl friend. I replied to Danielle, giving her all the available information regarding the loss of Sunderland W 3977 and where it had been based here on Lough Erne. I also sent her a copy of my Donegal Corridor book.

On December 2008, I had another e-mail regarding Sunderland W3977, this time from Wales in the U.K.

Dear Mr. O'Loughlin,

I found your website while looking for info about my mother's brother, P/O John Bartlett, who died at Loch Erne on 5th February 1942. I wonder whether you have any information about this or any photographs etc, – any thing which might relate to it. I have a quiet plan to bring my mother to Loch Erne some time in 2009 and would be grateful for any suggestions you may think helpful!

John apparently used to send home drawings/water colours he'd done in Ireland, which Mum remembers well.

Kind regards,
Dr. Anny Pritchard.

I sent Dr. Pritchard all the available information on Sunderland W3977, and arranged to send a copy of the Donegal book to her mother, Mollie Pritchard, for Christmas. In May 2010, after a lot of planning, six members of the Pritchard family came on a visit to Fermanagh and Castle Archdale, Robert, Mollie and Hugh, Anny, Shirley and Glynn. I had the pleasure of their company for the day and brought them to all the places of interest, including the war graves in Irvinestown. We also went to the coast at Bundoran, where they could see Donegal Bay and part of the Donegal Corridor that John would have flown along in his Sunderland.

In the words of a family member, "The visit to the beautiful country where John had served and the trips to various sites made it all come alive for us. A chapter of family history has finally been closed".

The six members of the family were all so appreciative of the help they received during this memorable visit. Sadly about a year later I had a letter from Mollie Pritchard to tell me that her husband, Hugh, had passed away.

The story of Sunderland W 3977 was not to end just yet. On 9th July 2009, I received an e-mail from a Jon Barker. He also had been recommended to me by George Smith.

"I have been given an updated e-mail address for you from George Smith. He hopes, as I do, that you can help me. I am seeking details of my 2nd cousin's father – Flt. Lt. Francis Wilfred Smith who crashed with all his crew off Malin Head (near Rathlin O'Birne Island – not the other Rathlin Is. Off Co. Antrim – this confused me for a while!) I'm trying to see if there is any other information regarding this particular tragic crash. It appears they were returning from a patrol when it happened. Is there any known cause? Is the exact crash site known?

I would like to buy a copy of your book "Voices of the Donegal Corridor". Any further bibliography about 201 Squadron, Castle Archdale or the role of the Short Sunderland would be most appreciated.

With my best wishes and thanks, Jon.

Jon Barker, (ex MN Radio Officer – (amongst other things). Tilehurst, Reading, Berks.

I sent Jon off a copy of the book and soon had a reply from him thanking me for the book, and for the e-mails with the details of W 3977.

He said, *"It is quite amazing what has turned up over the past couple of weeks since I was determined to find out more about my cousin's father, Flt.Lt. Francis W. Smith of 201 Squadron. I will continue my research, so if I find anything you (or George) might be interested in, I promise to forward it to you. I'm also in contact with Stephan Pullar, who is researching his own Great-Grand father who was killed when a dinghy capsized near Castle Archdale. It was he who gave me your and George's names and website – I owe all this new info to him! Has he contacted you – re his G-G- father?"*

There are no details as to what caused W3977 to crash. No May Day message was received at Castle Archdale. Was the explosion heard by the men in the Look-out post the cause of the crash, or did the plane explode when it hit the water and depth charges detonated? This we shall never know.

On receiving an e-mail from Stephan Pullar, I contacted my friend James Stewart, who is a leading expert on the history of the Flying Boats on Lough Erne. James kindly gave me the following information.

On 14th October 1942, a pinace boat of 201 Squadron, with maintenance crewmen on board, was lost when the boat capsized on Lough Erne. There were eight men listed as being lost from 201 Squadron. Lac. Francis Hart aged 28; Cpl. Frank Stafford; ACI Walter James Lanham aged 21; AC2 John Smith Falconer Thomson; AC1 Robert McAndrew aged 21; **AC1 David Pullar aged 27;** AC2 Owen Edwards, aged 21; and LAC William John Thomas aged 30.

Two other RAF men are listed in the Commonwealth War Graves Register (C.W.G.R.) for 14th October, 1942, Cpl. John M. Butchart and AC2 William Arthur Barton. They may also have been on the boat and their bodies never recovered.

Sunderland DD848 and other crashes on Mt. Brandon, Co. Kerry

There were four World War 2 air craft crashes on Mount Brandon, Co. Kerry. The first of these was that of a German Luftwaffe Focke-Wulf FW 200, which crashed on Faha Ridge, Mt. Brandon, on 20th August, 1940. The crew of six all survived and were the first German internees in the Curragh prisoner of war camp, Co. Kildare.

The second crash was that of Short Sunderland G-Ages, a B.O.A.C civilian version of the plane. It was on a flight from Lisbon to Poole in Dorset via Foynes on the Shannon, on 28th July 1943, when it crashed at 4-30 am on Sleiveglass, Mt. Brandon, Dingle, Co. Kerry. On board were seven crew and eighteen passengers, some were military and others civilians.

The third crash, on 22nd August, 1943, was that of Castle Archdale based Sunderland DD848. It also crashed at Sleiveglass. Eight of the crew died and three survived.

The fourth crash was that of a Vickers Wellington HE 208. It also happened at Sleiveglass, Mt. Brandon. All six of the crew, who were Polish members of the R.A.F., died.

The crew of G-ages were seven R.A.F. personnel: Capt. Tom Allitt aged 32; Second Officer John Harold Slater; N/O Eric William Vincent; E/O Harold Albert Victor Rawlinson; F/O Ralph Bousquet Lawes; R/O Charles H.P. Phillips; and R/O Frederick Thomas Parr. All survived except the Captain, Tom Allitt. One of the passengers who died was army Capt. Diarmuid John Hartigan, who was a native of nearby Buff, in Co. Limerick. Over 65 years later, a link was to be established between Katie Frazer, daughter of Tom Allitt, and Maureen Ingram, daughter of F/O Guy Wilkinson, the pilot of Sunderland DD848, who also died on Mt. Brandon. Katie and Maureen naturally had much in common to talk about.

Details of the final stage of the flight of G-ages are to be found in Donal MacCarron's book, 'Landfall Ireland', and in Jon Lakes book, 'Sunderland Squadrons of WW2'. Second Officer John Slater was at the controls when the Captain instructed him to alter course to 220 degrees. After a short time the Captain took over the controls to prepare for landing. He disengaged the autopilot, and started to descend at approximately 800 - 1,000 feet per minute. Suddenly, the ground was seen in close proximity, although the air craft was still flying in cloud. The Captain levelled out the air craft, opened up the throttles to full power and ordered 'fully fine' for fuel. The Second Officer obeyed the order; the Captain pulled back the control column in an attempt to climb. About 4 to 5 seconds later, the air craft crashed on Sleiveglass. It appears the starboard wing struck the mountain side causing the starboard engine to fall out. Donal MacCarron, in his book, gives a quotation from one of the passengers, Sgt. Alfred Brooker Depree, who was a pilot with the Royal New Zealand Air Force (R.N.Z.A.F.). He said that the pilot had put all four engines through the throttle range to boost power in an attempt to clear the ground. Without this action by the pilot, the aircraft would have impacted with greater force and possibly all aboard would have perished. The evidence of the Second Officer, John Slater, was very important. He died in 1986, Frederick Parr died 1989, and Sgt. Oliver Frith died 1996.

Causes for the crash were recorded as a 'Night effect,' which affected the accuracy of the direction finder apparatus in the aircraft; a strong south westerly wind, which resulted in the aircraft arriving at Shannon 30 minutes early; and a change in wind direction from South West to North West in the Shannon area at arrival time.

When Capt. Tom Allitt died in 1943, his daughter Katie was just 2 years and six months old. Less than a month after the loss of G-ages, F/O Guy Wilkinson lost his life in the crash of Sunderland DD 848 in the same place. His daughter, Maureen, was just an infant when he died. It was to be over 60 years before both girls learned the facts of how their fathers had died. Both of them had a son. Maureen's story is documented in the Donegal Corridor book.

F/Lt. Charles Seymour Grossey; F/Lt. Arthur Charles Griffin; Fl. Sgt. Norman Baron Pickford; Fl. Sgt. Joseph William Burton; Fl. Sgt. John Robert Coster; Fl. Sgt. Walter Noel Pitts; and Sgt. George Frederick Walter Tilt, were the crew members of Sunderland DD 848, who died in the crash. Sgt. George William Darkes, Sgt. John Sidney Applegate and Fl. Sgt. William

Mclean survived.

Katie Frazer and her husband, Graham, visited Kerry and the village of Cloghane, in 2007, and there met local people who had assisted at the crash. She also saw the memorial plaques erected in the village in memory of the crews who died in the four crashes. She returned again in 2009, and with Dennis Burke, climbed to the crash site of G-ages. Katie had discovered the websites of George Smith and Dennis Burke. There she learned of the existence of Maureen Ingram, and became anxious to contact her. Dennis introduced Katie to me, and in turn I was able to put her in contact with Maureen.

Katie's grandmother was from Tipperary, so there was a strong Irish influence in her life. In Kerry, Katie met Stella Grogan, whose husband, Rick, had been one of the stretcher bearers who brought Tom's body down the mountain. When Stella and Rick were married, they had been given a present of a Belleek Parian China cake plate. Stella decided to present the plate to Katie, who said, "Stella touched my heart by giving me a lovely Belleek China plate, which had been a wedding present to them, and telling me that she and Rick had always remembered my Dad in their prayers". Once again by some strange reason, my home village of Belleek comes into another picture of World War 2 events.

After years of imagining what might have caused the crash, and not knowing how her Dad had died, Katie learned all the facts about the crash as a result of information given her by George Smith and Dennis Burke. This brought her great peace of mind, and when she would visit her father's grave near Liverpool, she felt very close to him. As did Maureen Ingram, she obtained a die cast scale model of a Sunderland, which is, for her, a treasured possession. I also sent her a copy of the Donegal book, which she was delighted to have.

CHAPTER 2

Why does Nana Cry?

The final flight of Sunderland DW110

I have chosen this story for a variety of reasons, not least being the fact that Dyan Tucker, who lost her cousin Maurice Vincent Wareing in the crash (he was also her Godfather), penned, at my request, a poem to be read at a memorial service at the crash site. Dyan now lives in North Island New Zealand, and contacted me several years ago through Dennis Burke. Dyan has, along with Dennis, carried out intensive research which uncovered a great amount of information on the crash, and they have made contact with most of the families of the crew. Plans were made to hold a service on the Blue Stack Mountain in Co. Donegal, Ireland where Sunderland DW110 had crashed on 31st January 1944. The last known living survivor of the crash, Jim Gilchrist had died on 31st January 2008, the exact anniversary of the crash. Plans were made to have a memorial service on the crash site on Saturday, 31st May, 2008. The ceremony was filmed by Ulster Television, with their leading news reader, Paul Clark, giving a commentary on the proceedings. Knowing how much Dyan would have loved to be present, and being aware that this was not possible, I suggested that she might send a message to be read at the ceremony on behalf of the Wareing family. She penned the poem, *"Why Does Nana Cry?"* When I got the poem I passed it on to Paul Clark, asking him if he would kindly read it at the service. Paul told me later, that he found the poem so poignant and touching for himself and everybody present, that, due to his emotions, he found it difficult to read the poem.

To choose the lead story for this book was not an easy decision to make. Each and every crash was most important in its own right. The crash of

Sunderland DW110 was one of the most documented crashes of World War 2 planes in Eire, as the country was then named. It is not my intention to rewrite the story of DW110, but rather to record information that has come to hand in later years. When writing the *"Donegal Corridor"* book I did not know the connection DW110 had with Castle Archdale, so I now include it in this book.

The publicity given to this crash was due to a number of reasons. While serving in Donegal Town, Garda Liam Briody became aware of this crash. When appointed Sergeant in the town of Glenties in 1967, he was to meet with a number of people who had actually assisted in rescuing survivors of the crash, and also helped to recover the bodies of those who died. After intensive research, he published a book, *"The World War 2 Aeroplane Crash in the Blue Stack Mountains"*. This excellent history of the crash of Sunderland DW110 was the best record of one of the many crashes that happened in Eire during the war. There were 40 crashes in Co. Donegal alone, and about 200 in neutral Eire, details of each are recorded on Dennis Burke's website. Following publication of Liam Briody's book, a documentary titled *"The Last Flight of Sunderland DW110"* was filmed and broadcast on television.

In the early stages of his research, Liam Briody was put in touch with Gary Pentland of Gortin, Co. Tyrone. This was to prove to be an important factor in the search for information. Gary had a deep interest in World War 2 crashes and had become an expert on the subject. He had, with some friends, worked on the placing of memorials on a number of crash sites throughout the island of Ireland, one as far away as Clare Island in the west of Ireland Gary's son Ian, an enthusiast on aviation, placed advertisements in several aviation journals. There were some favourable results, and then in September 1986, a major break through was made when Ian Pentland had a phone call from a survivor of the crash, former Sergeant Jim Gilchrist. Slowly but surely the story of DW110 unfolded, and plans were made to have a suitable permanent memorial plaque placed on the crash site on the Blue Stack Mountains. This was to replace a temporary one that was on the site for several years. Gary Pentland was the leading force behind the project. He was assisted in the early stages by Seamus Gormley of Enniskillen.

The Crash of Sunderland DW110

This flying boat of 228 Squadron, Coastal Command was based at Pembroke Dock in Wales. On the morning of Monday 31st January 1944, at 10:45, it set off to patrol the Atlantic in search of the dreaded U-boats, and to protect shipping convoys bringing vital supplies to Britain. The area to be patrolled included the Bay of Biscay and the Atlantic Ocean off the west coast of Ireland. The duration of a patrol could be up to 16 hours. The names of the twelve man crew were:

- The Captain, F/Lt. Howard Charles Armstrong
- F/O. Maurice Vincent Wareing
- F/Lt Maurice Leonard Gillingham
- F/O. Joseph George Trull
- Sgt. Cyril Robinson Greenwood
- F/Sgt. Frederick George Green, R.C.A.F.
- Sgt. John Ernest Parsons
- F/Sgt. Arthur Gowans
- W/O. John Bruce Richardson
- Sgt. Frederick Tom Copp
- Sgt. Charles Stanley Hobbs
- Sgt. James Kenneth Gilchrist

Apart from the young Canadian, Fred Green, all the others were in the R.A.F. Fred Green was a last minute replacement for Harold Holdsworth, a native of Northern Ireland, who was in hospital with an infection at the time. Harold replied to the advertisement placed in the papers by Gary Pentland, but he had not known who replaced him on DW110. Green was not part of the 'normal crew', most of which had been involved in the rescue of downed airmen in November for which Armstrong was awarded the D.F.C. At the end of its patrol, DW110 was instructed to divert to Castle Archdale, Lough Erne, Co. Fermanagh, as weather conditions at Pembroke Dock had deteriorated considerably. The plane was intended to enter the Donegal Corridor and fly along the River Erne to Castle Archdale. It gave its estimated time of arrival at Castle Archdale as 23:30. This was the last message received from DW110. This was only the second flight in DW110 for F/Lt. Armstrong and his crew. His usual plane was Sunderland DM679, which was not available at this time.

DM 679 survived the war and was struck off charge, (SOC) on 6th July 1945.

The island of Ireland has been likened to a saucer in layout, with high hills and mountains around the coast, and low lands along the rivers making their way to the sea. The crew had missed the entry point into the Donegal Corridor, and continued to fly northwards for a short time before turning eastwards in the direction of Lough Erne. This route took them across the high mountains of Donegal, where the plane crashed on the Blue Stack range. Sad to say, had they been about 30 feet higher they would have cleared the high ground. Inadequate altimeters have been blamed for this problem. The facts were that altimeters were set for the prevailing atmospheric conditions at the time and place of departure, and if conditions were different on return, the altimeter gave a false reading that was not near accurate. To make the situation worse, the weather conditions on the Donegal Mountains were very poor, with snow and rain reducing visibility.

As this was not a regular return route for aircraft from Lough Erne, local people heard the low flying plane heading for the mountains. Several of them heard the noise of the crash, and could see the flames of the burning wreck a long distance away on the sky line. There were then no roads near the mountain, the principal transport being the humble bicycle. There were no phones apart from those in police stations, doctor's surgeries, Post Offices and the homes of clergy. It was only when two survivors of the crash arrived at the McDermott home that the alarm was raised and a search party organised.

When Jim Gilchrist phoned Ian Pentland in September 1986, he gave him the following account of the crash:

He found himself lying on the ground near the wreck which was burning, and the sound of exploding ammunition. It was raining very heavy and he had no idea how he came out of the aircraft. Soon he was joined by Sgt. A. Gowans; thankfully neither of them had any very serious injuries. The two men rested and at dawn discovered that there were four other survivors some with serious injuries; Flight Engineer W/O J.B. Richardson; the Navigator, F/O Joe Trull;, Sgt. Cyril R. Greenwood; and Flight Engineer Sgt. C.S. Hobbs.

Sadly Sgt. Cyril Greenwood was to die at the site on the morning of 1st February before medical help could get to him, having suffered serious injuries. Being the least seriously injured, Sgt. Jim Gilchrist and Sgt. A. Gowans set off at dawn down the mountain. Before leaving, they left two flares taken from a Mae West life jacket with the survivors, so that they could give a signal to a rescue party when it would be heard coming up the mountain. It might have been a good idea for Gilchrist and Gowans to have brought a flare with them to alert the survivors that they had reached help, there being no other means of communication in those times. The two men followed a stream that eventually brought them to the McDermott cottage, where they arrived about 10:30 a.m. (It may have been later, as it is doubtful if they could have made the journey down the mountain in 3 hours.) Mrs. McDermott, who was a widow with a young family, sent her 16 year old son, Joe, to accompany Sgt. Gowans, both on bicycles, to report the crash to the Guards (Irish Police) at Brockagh. Sometime after they had left, Warrant Officer J.B. Richardson arrived at the McDermott home from the crash site. Back at the crash site the injured survivors had no idea if Gilchrist and Gowans had found help.

Apart from the time of the crash which was confirmed, other times are estimated, bearing in mind that British and Irish times were different, Britain using double summer time, and Ireland using single summer time. Even during the winter there may have been a difference of an hour in the times recorded. A report was compiled following an investigation carried out by senior officers into the crash. It was signed by Group Captain G.A. Bolland on 12th February 1944. Evidence would have been taken from the survivors. Sunderland DW110, being off course, could have been out of range of the radio stations in Co. Fermanagh at Dernacross, Magheramena and Castle Archdale.

When Sergeant Tadhg O'Connor, the officer in charge of Brockagh Garda station, got the details of the crash from crew member Sgt. Gowans, he immediately organised a rescue party which included District Nurse Breege Cannon, and by mid-day they were on their way to McDermott's in a hackney car. Accompanied by other people and members of the Local Defence Force, the rescue party made their way up the difficult mountain side to the crash site. It would have been at least mid-afternoon before they got there. Shortly afterwards they were joined by an army unit from Rockhill army base. In the unit were the Chaplain and a Medical Officer. The two injured air men were taken down the mountainside by stretcher bearers. On arrival at McDermott's, they were attended to by ladies from the local Red Cross unit. Five of the bodies were brought down to McDermott's, and as darkness was falling, it was decided to wait until the following morning to bring the bodies of the two remaining crew members down the mountain. The bodies of the pilot F/Lt. Armstrong and F/Lt. Gillingham were still in the cockpit.

In keeping with that lovely old Irish custom of 'Waking the Dead' whereby a corpse is never left alone after death when the neighbours sit through the night in the wake house, two local men stayed for the night at the crash site with the bodies of the two remaining dead air men.

The 1st of February is a very important day in Ireland, for it is the feast day of St. Bridget. On the night of 31st January, the age old tradition of making crosses from rushes is carried out in many Irish homes. These are known as St. Bridget's Crosses, and they are placed on the rafters of the thatched Irish cottages, and on the graves of family members.

The crash of DW110 will always be associated with the feast of St. Bridget. All seven bodies of the dead were laid out at McDermott's house, where they were prepared for burial by local women, before being placed in coffins and taken to Finner Camp, Ballyshannon. Members of the Irish army transported the seven coffins to the border at Belleek; where they were handed over to the R.A.F. with full military honours.

The injured had already been taken to Irvinestown by ambulance on 1st February. Three of the dead are buried in the war graves at the Church of Ireland cemetery in Irvinestown. They are: F/Lt. M. L. Gillingham, R.A.F.; F/Sgt. E. Copp, R.A.F.; and F/Sgt. Fred Green, R.C.A.F. The other four: F/Lt. Howard Armstrong; F/O. Maurice Vincent Wareing; Sgt. Cyril Greenwood; and F/Sgt. John Parsons, all R.A.F., were returned to their families in England and buried there.

The survivors were: Sgt. Jim Gilchrist; Sgt. A. Gowans; W/O. J. Richardson; Sgt. C. Hobbs; and F/O. Joe Trull. Sadly, Joe Trull was to loose his life when Sunderland ML782 crash landed at Mount Batten on 10th December 1944. (Only two airmen died in this crash) This would indicate that Joe Trull's injuries were not very severe, as he was able to return to duty within a reasonable time after the crash in the Blue Stacks. W/O John 'Tubby' Richardson went on to have a distinguished career, and was involved in the Berlin Airlift for which he was decorated. Hobbs never returned to flying, and little is known of Parsons, though research is on-going.

Much more information about the crash came to light when Dyan Tucker, second cousin of Maurice Vincent Wareing, who was her Godfather, started her research. Dyan now lives in North Island, New Zealand. Her Nana was born Hannah Ann Jones on 14th September 1893, and died on 14th November

1957, aged 64. Hannah married John Joseph (Jack) Kelly, whose father was a native of Queens County (Co. Laois), Eire. Their son John Maurice Kelly was Dyan's Dad, and Hannah was Dyan's Nana, and Godmother to Vincent. John Maurice Kelly served for a time during the war in the Signals Branch, R.E.M.E. (army), based at Ballymena, Co. Antrim, N. Ireland. There he was involved in the development of Radar. Hannah and Vincent were very close, and she took it very hard when the word came of his death. As the only grandchild of Hannah, Dyan and she became very close and great friends. Dyan was only four and a half years old when her cousin, and Godfather, was killed. In 1982 Dyan and her late husband made several visits to Ireland, but not being familiar with the crash site did not manage to go to it. Her Dad, who was like a brother to Maurice, tried in vain to find out details of the accident, but he died without really knowing what had happened, as the internet had not been "invented" then, and information was "classified" for many years. Dyan went to New Zealand when she was in her twenties. There, she worked with a motor racing group. Her Dad and Mum joined her in 1991 and her Dad died in 1993.

It was in April 2008 that Dyan, searching in Google, discovered the website of the late George Smith, ex R.A.F., then living on Jersey Island. He had served for a number of years at Castle Archdale as ground crew. George sent a copy of Dyan's e-mail to me, and I then made contact with Dyan. She had already been in contact with Dennis Burke, a noted authority on World War 2 plane crashes in neutral Ireland. From him, she received a detailed history of the crash of DW110, details that she had spent years searching for, and information on other members of the Wareing family who had served in the war.

Other Sunderland's were diverted to Castle Archdale on the fateful day,1 2 1944 one of them DD847 landed safely on Lough Erne at 18:15. Another pilot, D.A. Sinclair, who had taken up residence in Australia, told how, as Captain of Sunderland JM683 of 461 Squadron, he was diverted to Castle Archdale. He had to fly up the west coast of Ireland, find Donegal Bay and enter the Donegal Corridor. He had not been issued with Wireless Telegraph crystal suitable for Castle Archdale, and so his navigator had to plot the course by dead reckoning. Captain Sinclair had flown past Donegal Bay, and discovering his mistake, turned back south to find the entrance to the Donegal Corridor. He said that in normal circumstances this would have posed no great problem. But the night was far from normal; the weather was the worst he had ever experienced, with exceptionally strong winds. Contact with the ground station was poor, but eventually they got enough information to let them know they were a long way north, and off course. The ground station was probably the RAF radio station at Dernacross, south west of Belleek. There was also an American radio station at Magheramena, about two miles east of Belleek. Captain Sinclair was aware that there was a very large altimeter error, due to the change in barometric pressure since take off. He had been air borne for 14 1/2 hours by this time. Now knowing that Lough Erne was approximately south, Captain Sinclair set off directly overland, at 4,000 feet. Shortly after crossing the coast, he found that cloud was forming below. He decided that this was not for him, and turned back to coast crawl, to find the entrance to the Donegal Corridor, which he did and landed successfully.

I do have an advantage over other historians and researchers into WW2 crashes, in the fact that I lived through those years. I have been to several crash sites within a short time after they happened, and I have spoken to survivors. I have listened to men giving 'eye witness' accounts of the conduct of people on the crash sites. (Some of these men had been nowhere near the crash immediately after it happened, and their accounts were without foundation.) Over the years, Dyan and Dennis did a tremendous amount of research and traced relations of most of the crew members, as listed below.

F/Lt. H.C.S. Armstrong D.F.C.:+   Dyan traced his family and his grave.

F/Lt. M.L. Gillingham: +*   Dyan traced a sister and niece, Heather Long. Gillingham was a version of the German family name "Guggenheim" which was changed by Deed Poll.

F/O. M.V. Wareing: +   A relation of Dyan's, she had much information on Vince. He had been married to Joyce Robertson. They had a daughter, Theresa, who had two children, Claire and Stewart.

F/O. J.G. Trull: Died in the crash of another Sunderland, ML782, at Mount Battan air base on 10th December 1944. His parents and fiancé. Steve, a relation.

W/O. J.B. Richardson, D.F.C.:   His parents and family. His niece, Ann, and her husband, Ron Powell, attended the ceremony on the Blue Stacks on 31st

May 2008.

Sgt. C.S. Hobbs: His wife lived in London and he died about 1990.

Sgt. C.R. Greenwood: + His parents and family. He was known as 'Paddy'. On October 19th, Geoff Greenwood, nephew of Cyril, contacted Dyan, thanking her for an e-mail about DW110. He said, "Thank you for the reply; it was just by accident that I came across your website. I will pass your site on to my cousins. It was only last year after a funeral that we started to find out about the air crash. We knew it was in Ireland, but not the location or the reason for the crash."

F/Sgt. F.G. Green, RCAF: +*   Dyan contacted his daughter, Carol Best, (husband Jim), in Canada. Following information from her uncle Harold Green. Fred was not a usual member of the crew. He had replaced Harold Holdsworth, who was ill.

Sgt. J.E. Parsons: + Parents and family.

Sgt. F.T. Copp: +*   Parents and family. Glynn Nation, a great nephew of Fred's.

Sgt. J.K. Gilchrist: Remained in the air force after the war and reached the rank of Squadron Leader in air traffic control, before retiring. He died 31st January 2008. On Saturday, 31st May 2008, his son James, who came from Winnipeg, Canada, and other family members, Adrian, Caroline, Sarah and Susan, attended the ceremony in memory of Jim and his crew, the ceremony being filmed by U.T.V.'s Paul Clark.

F/Sgt. A. Gowans: Died in 1975. Heather, a niece. Wife and son, Nick Gowans, who contacted Dennis in Oct. 2008.
Those who died are noted with +
Those buried in Irvinestown are noted *

On the 15th August 2007, the late George Smith received this e- mail from Andrew Johnston.

"Hello my name is Andrew Johnston. I have just found your website which is very interesting. I have only recently been investigating the circumstances surrounding the loss of Sunderland DW110 which crashed on the Bluestack in Jan. 1944. My uncle Cyril Greenwood was the wireless operator/air gunner and sadly was not one of the survivors. Have you any contacts from relations about this particular event? Regards Andrew".

George passed the message to me and I replied to it.

****

At 10 am sixty years ago today.
Twelve men left Pembroke Dock for Biscay Bay.
Little did they know that seven would not come home,
And families across the world would be alone.

Year by year the others passed away too, now they have all gone.
Jim Gilchrist passed away one year today; he was the very last one.
So raise your glasses as would have been their wish
And drink a toast to those we loved and miss.

For they were our heroes – those brave few
Who were Sunderland DW110's last crew.

Dyan Tucker, Paeroa, New Zealand.

****

To get full details of the crew of Sunderland DW110, and the crash go to Dyan's website www.freewebs.com/dw110.

Dennis Burke, who has given wonderful assistance to Dyan in her research, can be contacted at www.skynet.ie/~dan/war/crashes.htm
The late Sgt. George Smith of Jersey Island was another great source of information. His website www.sgt-george-smith.co.uk is still active. George served on the ground staff with the RAF at Castle Archdale.

Dyan has submitted the following message to readers of the story.

I would like to thank all those involved who have helped piece together what has been a mystery to me for many years, particularly Dennis Burke, for his research and photos, and Joe O'Loughlin, for his support and encouragement in my search. Also members of the R.A.F. Command Message Board, who have been so helpful, and also to the late George Smith for his help. To Paul Clark from Ulster Television who has helped keep the memory alive along with the people of the Blue Stack Mountains, the Ramblers and the good folk of Donegal. With special thanks to Gary Pentland and all his helpers for placing the Plaque in the Rock. Also to the family members who have shared their stories of their loved ones with us all and given us all the extra information and insight about that awful night. May God Bless and keep you all.

Dyan Tucker – cousin of F/O M.V. Wareing

John Quinn of Belfast, and local people, had painted a while cross and the outline of a Sunderland on the face of a rock near the crash site. An engraved metal plaque was inserted into the rock face by Gary Pentland and his son, of Gortin, Co. Tyrone, Michael Gallagher and his son Adrian, from Omagh, Seamus Gormley from Enniskillen, and local men Liam Briody and Joe McDermott. Seamus Gormley supplied a disc cutter and Milligan Brothers lent a generator. All this equipment had to be carried up the mountain. The plaque was unveiled by James Gilchrist on 9th September 1988. Sadly, Adrian Gallagher lost his life in the terrible bomb in Omagh on 15th August 1998. Gary Pentland has placed memorials on at least ten crash sites all over Ireland, including one in Co. Mayo on the west coast of Ireland. (A suitable plaque in memory of Adrian Gallagher has also been placed on the Blue Stacks site.)

During the course of our correspondence Dyan told me an unusual story. She and her husband had placed their house on the market in New Zealand.

"I am not sure if any of you believe in this, but we had a lady come around to view the house, who was a medium. Now, I am not a sceptic, but she was drawn to the photo of Vince that I have on the shelf above my computer, plus a couple of 'bits' of DW110 in a shadow box, with a photograph of the Sunderland in flight. She said to me "I am sorry to do this but can I tell you something"? and I said, 'Yes go on' (thought here we go!!) She proceeded to

tell me that all the "three Maurice's were reunited now" (Vince was Maurice Vincent, my Dad was Maurice, he died in 1993, and their uncle was Maurice, he died as an infant).

That knocked me back, there is nothing to indicate names, next came the fact that she said the "crew" were pleased that we had found them and they were all united again. Then she proceeded to tell me about the crash in detail and time- she said, winter time there was snow on the ground, not long before the end of the war, place-she said mountainside not in a "foreign" country but not in England, near a lake and they were off course and that there was a fire. She said that some survived and one died later in the same aircraft. That really spooked me".

Now there is nothing here that would give her any clues, so if she is right and if you believe in this sort of thing, perhaps the "boys" are watching us and looking down on us. Carol - she also picked up the fact that your Dad was not from the U.K. and said "He should not have been there" (which is correct in that he was a replacement for Holdsworth). She also picked up that Jim was the last to go in her words very recently, her exact words were "That the last crew member died in the last couple of years on a special date". By this time I was really getting upset and she stopped, but she has given me her name and said that if I felt like contacting her she would love to tell me more. I will think about it. She had no way of knowing any of these facts as she was from out of town and I had never seen her before in my life and the Real Estate Agent just brought her round on a "tour" of properties. There are other photos of my Mum, Dad, Grandma and a couple of friends (all gone now) on the shelf, but she went straight to Vince. Any way after I have spooked you all – let's take it for what it is, the "boys" are happy and we should be too.

This e-mail to me was dated 25th June 2010.

I was most impressed by this account, mainly because myself and other people who were researching crashes, got details from unexpected sources in several cases, and we all felt that the many "boys" are happy in the great here-after, and they were using us by some spiritual influence as instruments to let their families know how they died and that they were now in a happy place.

WHY DOES NANA CRY?

As we come together on this special day
My thoughts are with you from far away
Thanks to all for remembering the crew,
Who into this mountain in bad weather flew.

The Crew came from countrywide and over the Atlantic too.
They were the ones Churchill called "those brave few"
They were from two two eight squadron, Coastal Command
That kept us safe, as they flew over sea and land.

Some rest now in foreign fields, others in their homeland
But they will always be known as the crew of THE Sunderland
Their families will always be grateful to one and all,
Who remember their men folk here on the Mountain in Donegal.

From my family came Flying Officer Vince Wareing,
He was dark and handsome and Oh so caring.
His picture sat on the Welsh dresser, in a frame,
The family waited for him to come back, but he never came.

When the news came in forty four
All there was, a knock at the door.
Grandpa gasped and Nana cried,
All we knew was that Vince had died.

I never knew, where or how or when,
But I was only little then.
Vince was young, just twenty eight,
Grandpa, Uncle, and Dad lost their best mate.

His family never got over the shock,
They never knew about the plaque in the rock.
I often watched my Nana look to the sky,
And wondered, Why does my Nana cry?

Now the crew is finally complete,
Jim Gilchrist has taken the last seat.
The engines start up and all systems are go,
For the last mission of DW 110

The radio crackles and a voice is heard, "DW110 calling Heavens Gate
Permission to land Sir, sorry we're late"
Let us thank God that they lived, not that they died
For now I know, why my Nana cried.

Dedicated to the Crew of Sunderland DW110 and to my Nana, Hannah Ann Kelly, Vince's Godmother.
Dyan Tucker, Paeroa, New Zealand.

****

They shall never grow old, as we that are left grow old:
Age shall not weary them, nor the years condemn
At the going down of the sun and in the morning
We will remember them.

Taken from the poem 'For the Fallen' by Laurence Binyon (1914)

CHAPTER 3

A True Story of Sunderland NJ 175

The story of Sergeant Charles (Chuck) Singer and the crash of Sunderland NJ 175, is told in a chapter of the book **"The Donegal Corridor"**. Due to the efforts of local people, Louis Emerson, Una and Jim McGarrigle, Gary Pentland, and others, the site had been marked by a steel post with a plaque containing the names of the three airmen who lost their lives on Saturday, 12th August 1944. In later years, a very dignified memorial stone with a large engraved plaque, was placed on the site where the town lands of Cashelard and Corlea meet. Members of 422 Squadron from Canada were present for the unveiling of the plaque. At that time, there was little or no contact with any surviving members of the crew. All this was to change in January 2002, when Breege McCusker, the Irvinstown historian and authority on the Flying Boats on Lough Erne, got an e-mail letting her know that Chuck Singer was alive and well, now living in Florida. The original official investigation into the crash of NJ175 blamed crew members for it. As a result of the visit of Chuck, along with his son Bob, and speaking to eye witnesses who were on the scene, much new information came to hand that cleared the pilot of any blame.

I received the following article from Chuck Singer, via e-mail. The article was written by a nephew of Bill Watson, Bill being childhood friends with Evan Campbell (Cam) Devine.

Another article about the Belleek crash

Campbell (Cam) Devine was my Uncle Bill Watson's, best friend during early school days in Grand Valley, Ontario. Cam was killed on August 12th 1944, when the Flying Boat he was piloting crashed in Ireland. I am including a notice of his death from the Grand Valley Star and Vidette, and a detailed account of the crash as remembered by Chuck Singer, one of Cam's flight crew.

From The Grand valley Star and Vidette, August, 1944

Another Grand Valley Boy Passes Overseas.
News of the death of another Grand valley boy overseas was received in town the latter part of last week. He was Flight Lieut. Campbell Devine, elder son of Dr. and Mrs. E.W. Devine of Orillia formerly of Grand valley. Campbell was born in Grand valley and moved with his parents to Orillia some years ago. His death occurred in Ireland on Aug. 12th and interment took place in Ireland. He was a chum and pal of the late P.O. Bill Watson of Grand Valley. Brief references to his death were made in the pulpits of Knox Presbyterian Church on Sunday morning and at the memorial service for the late P.O. Watson in Trinity United Church on Sunday afternoon. Besides his parents and one brother, Donald, the deceased leaves a widow and one child, all of Orillia. To the bereaved parents, brother, widow and child the sympathy of this community is extended. Full particulars regarding his death had not been received at the time of going to press.

Taken from THE BATTLE OF THE ATLANTIC Highlights from 422 R.C.A.F. Squadron, 1942-1945
August 12th 1944, saw the crash of Sunderland T of 422, in Donegal County, Ireland, just north of Belleek, Northern Ireland, shortly after take-off for an Atlantic patrol. The heavily loaded aircraft had suffered an engine failure and loss of propeller, and a crash landing was attempted on a relatively flat area. The skipper, F/L Cam Devine and two crew members died in the crash. The remainder of the crew received serious injuries and were initially treated in the Irish hospital in Ballyshannon, Donegal County, and later moved to the military hospital in Necarne Castle near Irvinestown, Northern Ireland, or to hospitals in England.

Taken from "The Impartial Reporter" For Fermanagh, Tyrone and Border counties of the Republic of Ireland. Issue 15-08 2002
A tear ran down the cheek of Chuck Singer as he stood on the windswept bog land of Cashelard, receiving long overdue recognition for an act of great

courage undertaken 58 years ago today. It was a marvellous moment, a fitting closure to a remarkable tale, owing much not only to Chuck, whose selfless actions as a 19 year old First Gunner on a stricken Sunderland flying boat in 1944 saved the life of a comrade. A great day for his son Bob (who correctly pointed out that reports of his father's death in the Squadron records were greatly exaggerated), and local historians, Joe O'Loughlin and Breege McCusker.

A large crowd gathered on Monday at the exact hour at the site where Sunderland NJ175 crashed shortly after take-off from its base at Castle Archdale. They gathered to pay tribute to Sergeant Chuck Singer, and also to the three airmen who did not survive the crash, and whose names are recorded on a memorial stone erected at the site two years ago. With a beautiful ceremony choreographed brilliantly by Joe and Breege, interspersed with presentations to Chuck, the crowd listened to a recounting of the Canadian's remarkable story.

422 Squadron Royal Canadian Air Force arrived in Fermanagh in the spring of 1944, youthful, joyful crews of men, who had thus far generally enjoyed their war experiences, stationed with Coastal Command in Scotland, protecting Merchant Navy convoys from the threat of German U-boats. They were to do the same job from their base on Lough Erne, patrolling out into the Atlantic, and also into the Bay of Biscay and the English Channel. Their role was an important one; the U-boats were the only cog of the German war machine which really frightened Churchill, and any break in the Allies supply line would have had a debilitating effect on the war effort.

But to the airmen based in quiet Co. Fermanagh, on the usually serene Lower Lough Erne, the war must often have seemed a world away. Chuck remembers that conditions on the base were "beautiful, just fine", and that even when they were airborne, patrolling at an average altitude of 400 feet, there was never any real feeling of unease or fear. "We felt like nothing was ever going to happen to us out here. To fly was just a treat to get up, and if they ever postponed a flight on us we got sick, you know, just sick. I don't know any air crew that ever worried, it was all jovial, funny guys that had a good time, I don't know anybody that was worried about dying. Flying out to sea in those things was so peaceful. You almost forgot that you had a job to do, it was so beautiful and peaceful. During his short spell in Fermanagh, Chuck fortunately never had to fire his guns in anger from his position in the turret at the top of the giant seaplane, but he remembers one occasion when his crew felt they were about to have their first serious engagement with the enemy.

"We thought we had a pair of them, one time," he said. "It looked like a mother ship refuelling a smaller sub, so we dived at that thing, we had the depth charges out on the wings, we were ready for everything... and they were two of the most beautiful Blue Whales you ever saw in your life." Chuck left his turret and aimed a camera instead of his machine gun. He took a couple of photographs and left them in to get developed back at the base, but due to his most unfortunate exit from Castle Archdale he was never able to pick them up again. "We went out feet first and I never did get them. I'd loved to have had those pictures," he said wistfully.

The biggest threat to their safety that Chuck encountered during the patrols actually came from the Merchant Navy, which the Sunderland's and Catalina's were sent to protect. Engagements with enemy aircraft and U-boats were rare by 1944, but the Merchant convoys were jumpy, and fairly 'trigger happy', recalled Chuck. "The worst part was flying along side a convoy, because those merchant people – they were shooting at everything, and they didn't know us from the enemy. When we used to approach a convoy, the skipper used to give them every view they could of the markings, or else the Merchant Navy would shoot you down". They would also shoot coloured flares by way of identifying themselves, but the colours were changed frequently, and sending up the wrong colour could prove fatal. Call signs were also used for identification, and changed frequently, but there is one call sign which is indelibly printed in Chuck's memory. 'Eyeglass Eagle'. This was the last call sign of Sunderland NJ175, as it took off around 11:15 on Saturday morning, August 12th, 1944. NJ175 was like any other Sunderland docked at the Flying Boat Base, and was supposed to have been checked by the engineers before take off. Every one of the twelve man crew had checks to make after being rowed out to the boat on a dinghy.

"When it was our turn to fly, they'd put us in a dinghy from the dock and run us to one of the boats, and we'd get in and check every thing out, and if some thing wasn't right we'd radio the dinghy and it would come back and get us and take us to another one. Often there'd be two or three before we'd get one that was operational." Every thing happened in such a hurry that it was fairly common to experience mechanical problems", said Chuck, "and often the crews would be delayed at least an hour by repairs. On the flight of August 12 was his regular crew, all of whom had got to know each other like brothers, having flown and socialised together in Fermanagh for months, as well as a few trainees, learning the ropes, and sitting, fatally as it turned out, near the cockpit behind the skipper, Flight Lieutenant Cam Devine.

They were heading for the English Channel, hoping to catch the German subs heading for Norway from their base at Brest on the French coast. The men, all members of the Royal Canadian Air Force (R.C.A.F.), were expecting to be away for between 10 and 12 hours, burning an enormous 2,000 gallons of fuel. As it happens, they were only airborne for a fraction of that time, about 30 minutes, and had to dump as much of the fuel as possible over the surrounding area. "The engine sounded uneasy all the time after we took off, it didn't sound like it was hitting all cylinders, it sounded funny. Sometimes that clears up, but this time it didn't," said Chuck. The noises got worse as the plane reached the West Coast of Ireland, and a problem in the outer starboard engine had developed into a fire. The crew sent out a Mayday call, and turned around to return to base. Orders came in from Castle Archdale to jettison the fuel and the depth charges on board, which would have exploded on impact with the ground.

Local people in the fields around Belleek were used to seeing the huge Flying Boats flying out to war over their heads, along the secretly negotiated Donegal Corridor, but to see one with thick black smoke billowing out from its starboard engine was an unusual and alarming experience. Although Cashelard is a remote area, there were a number of people in the vicinity, taking advantage of the great weather to work in the fields or enjoy the first day of the Grouse shooting season. Their peace was soon to be shattered. On board the plane, dumping the 2,000 gallons of fuel was proving too dangerous, as the high octane fuel was pouring out perilously close to the burning engine, risking an explosion which would blow the plane to smithereens. Flying Officer Alex Platsko, the Second Pilot, whose job it was to jettison the fuel and depth charges in preparation for a less than routine landing, now had to shut off the fuel dump valve again. And there was another problem - the track for the depth charges was sticking, and the crew couldn't get them out of the plane. Eventually, after a desperate struggle, the crew worked the charges free, and they dropped harmless to the ground, to be blown up the next day by the Irish Army and officials from Castle Archdale.

Platsko returned to the task of shutting off the fuel dump valve, but was shuddered out of his work by a loud bang, as the burning engine suddenly froze up and the propeller twisted off its shaft and spun into the starboard float, causing the plane to bank suddenly, steeply, to the right. Chuck remembers the sharp snap of the propeller breaking off, not long before impact. Skipper Cam Devine, just 22 years of age, had a fight on his hands. With one engine on fire and out of action, and a half tonne propeller embedded in the side of one of his floats, the plane was loosing height at a frightening rate, and in danger of hitting the ground sideways first. "We could've cart-wheeled; if the wing had touched first we would all have been dead," said Chuck. The crew members were adopting crash position, something similar to what is advised on commercial airlines today, but without the fancy demonstration cards. Cam Devine was fighting for his life, and the lives of his comrades, fighting to get the heavy plane back on an even keel to give them a chance in the crash landing. which was inevitable. Somehow, against the odds, he achieved this, righting the plane just before impact on the Cashelard ground, succeeding in saving the lives of nine of his crew members, but losing his own life in the process.

Chuck remembers certain aspects of the impact, but he was concussed, and blood was streaming down his face. Three of the crew - Cam Devine, Pilot Officer R.T. Wilkinson, and Flight Sergeant Jack Forrest, - died instantly. Alex Plastko, who hadn't time to buckle himself back into his seat after jettisoning the depth charges, was thrown through the windscreen, and survived, although he was seriously injured. The plane hit the lip of a country track, coming down perpendicular to the road rather than along it, which caused the bottom half of the plane to be severed in the sudden halt. "When the bottom half of the plane was torn out, I was up in the ceiling getting my arms broke and my face cut, and concussion, and I was looking down and I could see George Colbourne laying face-up on the bottom of the boat," recalled Chuck. "We went over the top of him, but it looked like we were still and he was sliding on a toboggan underneath us; that was the effect we got. That was the last thing I remembered until I regained consciousness again, and tried to get out of that thing".

The next thing Chuck remembers is the heather all around the crash site being on fire. The Sunderland had broken in two places, at the tail, and between the under section and the rest of the plane. The tail breaking off was a blessing in disguise, affording an escape hatch for Chuck and some of the other crew members. Dazed, bleeding, and with his left arm hanging limply by his side, Chuck some how got out of the mangled remains of the plane. As aviation fuel leaked out of the plane, the fire spread, and bullets and ammunition were exploding in the heat. Chuck staggered clear of the heat, but heard George Colbourne crying for help. George was trapped under the wreckage of the tail, powerless, with two broken legs. Chuck turned back into the flames. "I can remember going back when I heard him crying and screaming. I heard him before this, and I thought 'God, I'm not going to get him', and then he screamed one more time and I thought, 'I've got to get to him', so I went back after him. I pulled my arm out hauling him out. I tore a ligament in my shoulder. I couldn't use my left arm, it was broken. So by the time I got him maybe 50 to 100 feet away, I don't know how far it was-until I couldn't feel the heat anymore. I passed out, and so did he.

The fire totally engulfed the plane, but somehow all of the survivors had got clear of the wreckage. Joe O'Loughlin reached the plane, (having run across the fields and mountain) about an hour after the crash, along with other locals and helpers, including the supposedly neutral Irish Army, from Finner Camp, rescue services from Castle Archdale, and medical staff from Ballyshannon's Sheil Hospital. The Doctor and Priest from Belleek. All the injured, with wounds ranging from a broken back to severe burns, were taken to the hospital, where they remained for 48 hours, before being transferred to St. Angelo Airport and over to hospital in England.

At this point, according to the records of 422 Squadron, Sergeant Charles (Chuck) Singer, died. This was quite an alarming discovery for his son, Bob Singer, in January 2002, who knew that his father, who had not fully recovered from his injuries, received a medical discharge and was flown back to Canada, where he later married, had five children and moved to Florida. Chuck kept in contact with George Colbourne, who rang him every year on August 12 to thank him for saving his life on a lonely Irish bog, a lifetime ago. Bob had decided to do a little research into his father's Air-force career, and had stumbled upon the squadron records. He knew very little of the crash, and nothing of his modest father's heroic rescue of Colbourne. He sent a reply to the website, stating that his father had been helping him in the yard that morning, and notwithstanding a Lazarus-like reincarnation, he had not died in England on August 14th, 1944, as the squadron notes reported. Chuck had missed out on over 50 years of squadron reunions thanks to an erroneous report in the records. He had no idea that there was such an interest in those based at Castle Archdale. "I didn't have a clue, I thought that we were all forgotten. Joe here, he got after me right-away, I got a letter within a week from him." Chuck also got in touch with the courageous Alex Platsko, now

Dr. Alex Platsko, who lives in the prestigious Pebble Beach resort in California. The two old comrades talked together for the first time in 58 years, a few months ago, (2002) while Chuck ordered his Squadron badge, an honour he had been deprived of for over half a century.

This has been a year of amazing discovery for both Chuck and Bob, who accompanied his father on his emotional return to Fermanagh and to Cashelard. Under the gentle guidance of Joe, they have revisited so many areas of huge significance for Chuck - the well kept war graves in Irvinestown, where his three comrades are buried, Castle Archdale, with Breege McCusker; the Sheil Hospital in Ballyshannon, where Chuck asked the staff if he owed anything and joked that he had 'an outstanding bill from 1944, and finally, most emotionally of all, the site at Cashelard, where Sunderland NJ175 crashed 58 years ago to the day. Full of praise for the people of Fermanagh and Donegal, "a wonderful race".

Chuck returns this week to Florida, laden with gifts such as a mounted piece of the wreckage of his plane, a citation commemorating his bravery, a copy of the memorial plaque erected to the memory of his fallen comrades, and a replica model of the plane, in which he soared above the seas, risking his tomorrow for our today. A special guest at the ceremony to meet with Chuck, was Dr. Edward Daly, Bishop of Derry, who as a young boy had cycled out to scene of the crash. Well over 200 guests attended the ceremony at the crash site. It was televised by UTV, broadcast on Radio, and reported in the local papers. The Irish army was represented by Commandant Sean Curran from Finner Camp, and an Irish air sea rescue helicopter did a fly past in tribute to Chuck and his comrades. The Cashelard Community Association provided refreshments for all the guests in the local pub.

Having been reacquainted with his squadron, and returned to the site of his wartime experiences, he admits to being over whelmed with his time in Fermanagh. As far as Castle Archdale, Cashelard and more particularly, Flying Boats go, he has just one disappointment, and he is not the only one. "It's a shame there isn't a flying boat for you guys to look at, you know? They're all at the bottom of the lake. Isn't that crazy?"

The above story was posted on Flickr.com/photos in March 2009. In a chapter in the Donegal Corridor book, "Sergeant Chuck Singer" tributes are paid to the many people who made the return visit of Chuck to Cashelard an outstanding and memorable event. Copies are still available from the author. Names of the crew not mentioned are: Sgt. Allen, Sgt. Jeal, whose family visited the scene in 2010, Sgt. Oderskirk, Sgt. Clarke, P/O A. Locke, and P/O Parker.

Some comments posted on www.Flickr.com/photos, the above mentioned website included: commented on the bravery of Cam Devine to get the plane upright to save the lives of others. I am glad Chuck finally got the recognition he deserved for his courage.

An amazing story of bravery and devotion to his comrades. This is wonderful, and thank you for sharing it with us. It is amazing how much information you were able to find. Just fascinating. What a wonderful tribute you have given to a brave pilot for his commitment.

This brave young pilot lives on in Flickr and what a great way to tell his story and that of the other young men, to think that he was only 22 – what an amazing tale.

An incredible and moving account – Bill. You really put in a lot of time and effort researching this and putting it all together for us to read.

Fascinating and moving to read the full story-thank you for posting such a detailed account. As the son of a Sunderland pilot who did come home, it strikes a particular chord with me.

Chuck Singer and his son, Bob, returned once again to Co. Fermanagh in September 2011, as special guests to partake in the Fermanagh Flying Boat Festival. Chuck was in great demand by all sections of the media, and made himself available to reporters anxious to record his part in World War 2. When Bob started his research in 2001, his Dad was after suffering the death of two of the most important people in his life, the death of his beloved wife, and his dear friend George Colbourne. The fact that Chuck then made contact with Alex Platsko, and in Ireland spoke to several eyewitnesses of the crash, ensured that the true story of the crash could be compiled, and the bravery of Cam Devine made known, and recorded, in the history of 422 Squadron. This is another chapter in the life of Sergeant Charles Singer R.C.A.F. In conclusion, let us salute those brave airmen who returned home when hostilities ended, and also those who now rest in well attended graves in Irvinstown cemeteries, and remember too the many who lie with their aircraft deep at sea in the Atlantic ocean, and have no known graves.

Dr.Al Platsko passed away in 2011.

CHAPTER 4

The Crash of Sunderland W3988
Doughmore, Doonbeg, Co. Clare

This Canadian Crew alas never knew,
As they toured over Erin's green shore,
That the very last deed of their faithful machine,
Would occur on the shore of Doughmore.

The opening lines of a recitation composed by two West Clare men to mark the arrival of the RAF Short Sunderland Mk 11 - Serial No.W3988 - name "Pluto". that crash landed in Doughmore Bay, Doonbeg, Co. Clare, on 3rd December 1941, about 18:30 hrs.

This was the first Sunderland flying boat to crash in neutral Eire (Ireland) since they were deployed to the Castle Archdale Base on Lough Erne, Co. Fermanagh, in October 1941. Sunderland W3988 took off early on the morning of December 3^{rd,} on a mission to find an allied shipping convoy, and give it protection from the dreaded German U-boats.

This part of the story was easy to assemble, but much of the remainder proved far more difficult. For a start, the West Clare composers were not correct in saying it had a Canadian Crew. The only Canadian on board was the Pilot, Flight Lieutenant James Grant Fleming. So what was the composition of the crew on this ill-fated flight?

As was normal for Flying Boats on long-range missions, there were three pilots; Flight Lt. Fleming, a Canadian, who enlisted in the Royal Air Force; Pilot Officer Wilfred Sefton Emmet, Royal New Zealand Air Force; and Pilot Officer Eric Gerald Marker, RAF. Flight. Lt. Fleming, aged 24, was the most senior officer, and Captain of the Mission. These three were assisted by; Sgt.

Eric Willows Jackson; Sgt. Sydney James Epps; A/Sgt. Maurice Walter Gerald Fox; A/Sgt. James Cannell Masterson; LAC Frederick Walter Lea; LAC Arthur Doncaster; LAC Andrew Patrick Walker; and AC Albert Everall Bennett. (All members of the R.A.F.)

Over the years many stories appeared in the media, and all invariably gave the "facts" as far as the author was concerned, but there were unexplained coincidences that suggested there was a fuller story if only one could find it. Then on February 17th 2012, came a eureka-style moment, when a file marked "Doughmore Crash – Dec. 1941" was discovered in the Military Archives in Dublin. This file provided over 150 reports, memorandum, hand written records, notes scribbled on location as aid memoirs, records of discussions with the pilot; an absolute treasure trove account of that fateful December 3rd on the shore of Doughmore, as the Atlantic waves tossed and drove the stricken aircraft into the bay. The file gives an interesting insight into the care and discipline of the authorities in dealing with even minor details, and the thoroughness they applied to recording and filing each relevant document, even the official instruction to open a file on the crash is found within the main cover.

So let the story begin with Flt.Lt. J.G. Fleming's account, extracted from his debrief statement after returning to active service following escape from the Curragh Detention Centre, where he enjoyed far greater hospitality than might have been his lot had he landed in Western Europe in December 1941. Others have written about life at the Curragh, Co. Kildare, and since this is about the crash of his aircraft, we shall not examine his life at the Curragh Holiday Camp.

James Grant Fleming was born in Calgary, Canada, on May 23rd 1917. In 1936, he was a Gunner in the Royal Canadian Artillery. In 1937, Fleming volunteered for the Royal Air Force Aircrew and was accepted as Acting Pilot Officer on Probation, January 9th 1938. Fleming successfully completed his air crew training, and was promoted to Flying Officer on May 30th 1940. He was assigned to Ferry Command, where he remained active from Dec. 1940 until Sept. 1941, when he was assigned to 201 Squadron, based at RAF Station, Sullon Voe in Shetland. In November 1941 he was promoted to Flight Lieutenant, and reassigned to 201 Squadron based at Castle Archdale on Lough Erne, Co. Fermanagh, N. Ireland. At this time, 201 Squadron was being re-equipped with Sunderland Mk 11 Flying boats. (Military Archives, Hendon, Middlesex, UK.)

About 4:00 am on Wednesday, Dec. 3rd, as captain of a Routine Mission, the newly promoted Flt. Lt. Fleming prepared his craft for take-off. He and two co-pilots, plus crew of eight, were assigned to Sunderland W3988. The flight took off from Lough Erne shortly after four on the morning of 3rd December 1941. Their mission was to find an Allies shipping convoy and give it protection from the dreaded German U-boats. Due to adverse weather conditions, they failed to locate the convoy, and they decided to return to base. According to Fleming the navigation equipment had failed, and they had strayed from the planned flight path. They were completely lost. With fuel running low, the pilot decided to look for a suitable place to land. About four o'clock, he identified what looked like a suitable bay, and then circled around in the hopes of finding a place where visibility was better. The weather didn't improve, fuel was now low, so at about 6:30pm he made his decision to land as close as possible to the coast, in the bay he had earlier identified. Local people later reported sightings near Doonbeg Bay about 4 o'clock in the afternoon, but that the plane headed north only to return to the area about six. Flt. Lt. Fleming stated in his debrief after his escape from detention and return to active service, that he decided to land soon after six o'clock, but he was not certain as to where he was heading. On touching the high waves the port float snapped. (U.K. Military Archives)

He took off again in an attempt to get a better approach and ordered his crew to standby for emergency evacuation. His second attempt at 18:30 hours was going well, until the port engine struck something, possibly a submerged rock, and broke off. This caused the aircraft to list heavily and made it difficult for the crew to abandon, but they all got away, except Bennett, Masterson and the pilot. The sea was very rough, and the wind was driving the flying boat before it, but they had no idea where they were heading.

Bennett could not swim, so Fleming kept him back so that Masterson would help him into the remaining rubber dinghy. Masterson entered the water holding the dinghy line, and as Bennett jumped, Masterson bundled him into the dinghy. Masterson was a powerful swimmer, and he rolled in with ease bur discovered the canvas had ripped and the boat was sinking fast. Fleming jumped last but saw the dinghy float away as he touched the water.

The three airmen then tried to find a bearing, and decided to swim with the roll of the wave. That should take them towards land. Masterson stripped off his uniform, in the knowledge that it would weigh him down as it soaked up the water. Anyway, he could help Bennett better without it. Within a short distance they felt soft sand beneath their feet, and were able to stand, with some difficulty, for long enough to get a better bearing. Masterson saw a faint light in the distance to his left. Then they saw a bright light that appeared to be scanning the water, and called in that direction, but got no reply, so they decided to swim towards it.

Unbeknown to the three airmen, there were three local men, Simon McCarthy, Michael Stack and Michael Stack Jnr., with a single carbide lamp scanning the waves for survivors. Simon had seen the aircraft earlier and felt it was in distress, so after returning from his work, went to the Stack cottage where the two Stack men joined him, and walked about one mile over rough terrain to reach the shore. While on their way, another local man, Michael O'Donovan, an L.D.F. soldier, enquired about the crash, saying he would have to report to his Commanding Officer. McCarthy explained that the aircraft was a flying boat and that it may not have crashed; it could make a safe landing in the bay. O'Donovan agreed that that was possible, and decided to follow the three to the shore, but went back home first. The three reached the shore close to the scene of the crash, and thought they heard the heavy drone of the engines and loud noise, but could not see anything. Then, due to a break in the cloud, they were certain they saw the fuselage high in the water and not far out. The ocean noise was far too loud to be able to pick up any calls for help, but they continued to scan the waves with their light. Then, suddenly, they saw two men, one of whom appeared to be helping his comrade.

Out at sea the three airmen moved off the sandbank towards the light, but within a very short distance, Bennett and Fleming disappeared into a deep hole. On seeing this, Masterson veered off and swam hard to his left to avoid being sucked in. He was an experienced fisherman who knew the hidden dangers the shore can conceal. He later said he remembered the light in the distance, and set his mind on it now that his colleagues had gone under.

However, there was still hope for Bennett and Fleming, because the men on shore had seen them and had entered the dangerous waters of the storm driven tide. Stack Snr, grabbed one man and hauled him ashore. That man was later identified as Flt. Lt. James Grant Fleming, the pilot, but as he slumped on the shore it was obvious he was in a poor state and needed resuscitation quickly. McCarthy had spent time in the U.S.A. and was trained in First Aid and survival techniques. He decided to attempt to revive the airman using the Prone Pressure technique but the sand was soft so he called to Stack Jnr. to fetch a flagstone to put under the man's chest. Using the stone as support, he began to apply prone pressure to the airman. After some time he noticed a small trickle of water flowing from the man's mouth, then he coughed and his body jerked suddenly; he was safe. While this was going on, a second man, later identified as AC1 Albert Everall Bennett (1081395) Royal Air Force, was pulled ashore and Stack Snr began to copy McCarthy's actions in an attempt to revive him.

Meanwhile, O'Donovan had got to the scene, and observed that two men were 'rescued' in his understanding, and he set off in a hurry to report the incident. He walked and cycled to the Doonbeg Garda Barracks, a distance of about 4 1/2 miles from where he witnessed the 'rescue'. The Duty Officer alerted the military in Kilrush.

By this stage, Stack Snr. was crouched beside Fleming on the shore talking to him and trying to keep him awake, as they did not want him to fall asleep. McCarthy was working on Bennett, and Stack Jun was holding the light. McCarthy continued with the attempted resuscitation, but on finding there was no pulse and no sign of life coming from Bennett, he made the sign of the cross on Bennett's forehead. He then took the lantern from Stack Jnr, and asked him to move the body further up the beach in case it got washed out to sea again, and began to scan for survivors. He had moved some distance along the water edge when Slack Snr called; "Simon, come here he (Fleming) is shivering and babbling".

Simon McCarthy recognised the symptoms of hypothermia and said to his partner, "We'd better get him under cover or he won't survive either". It was decided to take him to Stack's cottage. They got Fleming to his feet and moved towards the shore, then on to the very rough terrain of the bent-covered hills. Fleming stumbled, and became quite agitated, demanding to know where they were taking him. McCarthy explained his state, and said they were taking him to the home of the man who dragged him from the sea, where they would look after him. Fleming was not sure and appeared reluctant to go with them, understandable in the circumstances! Michael Stack Snr, a strong stocky man, picked Fleming up, put him across his shoulder and moved off at a brisk pace. They were soon at the cottage, and Fleming was given a cup of strong sweet tea, laced with a local spirit brew that is claimed to have secret healing powers, and wrapped him in blankets. Flt. Lt Fleming soon revived, but he was extremely lucky, because he was not long in the water and was rescued by men who knew how to revive him. He was soon talking and asked where he was. McCarthy replied; "You are in the Free State, rest, your war is over". On hearing this he swore and said. "Why didn't the old bitch take us to the Border?"

About 20:15 hours, 2nd Lieut. D. Spicer (Irish Army) called to the Stack cottage to check and interviewed Fleming, who refused to give any details apart from his personal identity. Documents showed his next of kin as Mr. Fleming (father) c/o Dr. S.C. Morris, Southern Buildings, Calgary, Canada. He was 24 years, and had completed two years service in the RAF. (Reference MH/293/41).

Lieut. Spicer listed and removed all official documents and objects from the air man, making a detailed list of each item, and giving Fleming a signed receipt. In the Officer's opinion, Fleming was suffering from shock. He was then allowed to rest until next morning, when he was transferred to the custody of the Irish Army. Before departing from the scene, Lieut. Spicer posted a Local Defence Force Guard on the house. (Reference G2.41/108)

While Fleming was enjoying the hospitality and attention of the Stack family, his colleague, James Masterson, was battling the Atlantic waves in his desire to reach the distant light he had seen soon after abandoning their plane. As mentioned, he was a powerful swimmer, and a man of great stamina. This all helped him reach his goal unaided, an amazing feat when one views that rugged shoreline even on a calm sunny day. On that dark winter night, it was truly heroic. When he reached the scene of the light, he discovered it was a substantial farmhouse perched right on the edge of the Atlantic. He knocked on the lighted window of Patrick Shanahan's house. Patrick's mother said she heard a noise at the window. Patrick and his brother John went to investigate, and found the scantily clothed Sgt. James Masterson. He was in a state of near exhaustion. The men helped him into the house, where they set about reviving him with hot drinks and sips of warm whiskey. The airman responded quickly, but he had suffered many cuts and bruises, especially to his legs, and he was in a state of shock. (Reference John Quealy, 'Down by the Chapel Gate in Cooraclare-Page 109)

After completing the formalities of interviewing Fleming, Lieut. D. Spicer set out for the homestead of Patrick Shanahan to interview another survivor recently reported to him by the authorities. A local man acted as guide, and travelled with him in an army truck to the Shanahan homestead. On arrival, he was greeted by Patrick, and introduced to Masterson. It was a very simple affair; the man had no possessions to record. He gave his next of kin as Mr.

William Masterson, Swanton Abbott, Norfolk, England. He was aged 24 years, and had completed two years service in the RAF. The Officer considered he was suffering from shock and noted cuts and abrasions on his legs, so after mounting a Local Defence Force Guard on the house, the airman was allowed to rest until next morning. The interview with Masterson is logged at 21:35. (Reference G2.41/108 and MH/294/41)

According to the official report filed next day (4th) by Major P. O'Connell, G2 Southern Command, the Pilot made a decision to land in Doughmore Bay, about 2 1/2 miles from Doonbeg, at 18:30 hrs. The craft hit a submerged rock that broke off the Port Engine. This caused the craft to list, but it continued into the bay before finally coming to rest less than half a mile off high water mark. The tide washed the fuselage to within 80 feet of high water mark later in the night, but one wing was missing. Lieut. D.D. Spicer, Army Cavalry Corps, Kilrush, was alerted by Michael O'Donovan, a member of the L.D.F., at 19:23 hrs. Due to earlier reports of an aircraft that appeared to be in distress, the military were on stand-by in the area, and a Military Party was on the scene by 19:55 hrs. One dead airman was located at 20:05 hrs. There were no civilians on the scene, and a cordon was deployed to ensure nobody attempted to approach the wreckage. Additional Local Defence Force men were called out to comb the surrounding countryside for any airmen that might have got ashore. None were found. (Reference S41/108)

Major O'Connell's report above, fits closely with notes made of Fleming's 'comments' while in hospital. He said he was the last to leave the stricken craft. He saw Masterson and Bennett in the water. They tried to use a rubber dinghy, already in the water, but it was washed away by the swell. Masterson was helping Bennett stay afloat, but Bennett was panicky. They saw a light and moved towards it. Bennett went under, although they could feel sand under their feet. He lost contact with Masterson at that point. Bennett was dragged ashore close to the same spot where local men rescued him (Fleming). One of the men tried to resuscitate Bennett but failed. The men took him to a house where he was given warm refreshments. (Reference S41/108)

In contrast with some local belief that some lives had been saved, the grim business of crew members bodies being washed a shore had to be handled with care and dignity. The bodies of AC1 Albert Everall Bennett and Lac Arthur Doncaster, were taken from the strand at Doughmore to the Slough Hall, Doonbeg, on the evening of Dec. 4th. They were buried the next day at

4:30pm, in the Church of Ireland Cemetery, Doonmore, Doonbeg, Co. Clare, with full military honours.

The British Representative to Eire was represented by Mr. G.W. G. Lywood. After the burial, Captain P. Daly (Irish Army) accompanied Mr. Lywood to the scene of the crash, and reported that he examined the keel of the craft. It would appear he was preparing a report on the likely cause of the crash. Mr. Lywood also enquired about the Flight Documentation, remarking "I suppose your people picked up these", (reference S41/108) Dated 9th Dec. 1941.

On Dec. 6th at 10:35am, the bodies of LAC Frederick Walter Lee and Sgt. Sydney James Epps were washed ashore about one mile west of Quilty, Co. Clare. They were buried in the Church of Ireland Cemetery, Miltown Malbay, Co. Clare, at 4:30pm on Sunday Dec. 7th, with full military honours. The British Legation was not represented at the funerals.

On Dec. 21st 1941, Anthony Shanahan, Quilty, reported to the local Garda that a body was washed ashore west of the town. The Garda went to the scene, and found a body wearing a jersey marked "Pluto", but with no other identification. The body was not identified, but was believed to be one of the crew of the Sunderland Flying Boat that crashed on Dec. 3rd in Doughmore Bay. The unidentified body was buried in the Church of Ireland Cemetery, Miltown Malbay, Co. Clare, on Dec. 22nd. (reference: Quilty Garda Incident Log) Four of the eleven crew members were never accounted for; Pilot Officer Wilfred Sefton Emmet, New Zealand Air Force; Pilot Officer Eric Gerald Marker; Sgt. Eric Willows Jackson; and LAC Andrew Patrick Walker, all Royal Air Force. The unidentified airman buried in the Miltown Malbay cemetery was very likely one of these four. It is surprising this man has not been identified; with the enormous advances in DNA profiling; it should not be a difficult exercise, as there are just four families involved.

On January 18th 1942, Thomas O'Boyle of Quilty discovered the body of Sgt. Maurice Walter Gerald Fox, RAF, on the shore off Mutten Island, and reported the sighting to the Garda. Quilty Garda notified the authorities, and the Kilrush Military Post was tasked with arranging the recovery and the funeral. Capt. P. Daly, and one Corporal, drove to Quilty, where they met with Mr. Boyle at the Garda Barracks. The sea was rough, but Tom O'Boyle and his fishing partner, John Kelleher, agreed to row to the island. Tom suggested two canoes were needed to transport the two military men, Garda Sgt. Hegarty, and the coffin, for a fee of 10 Shillings per Canoe. Capt. Daly would not agree, and said there was no need for the Garda to be involved. One canoe was launched, but an oar was broken due to the conditions. Later, when beaching at Mutten Island, a number of timber ribs were broken, and some of the canoe canvas was ripped, but the body was successfully recovered and brought to the mainland. The agreed fee of 10 Shillings was paid to Mr. Boyle for his services, and it was also agreed that he would submit a claim for the damage to his canoe, when he had a full estimate of the cost involved.

Following the recovery of the body, Captain P. Daly filed a report saying that both Boyle and Kelleher underwent considerable hardship that day, in launching and beaching the canoe. They also assisted with carrying the body about one mile across the rugged shore, to where it could be loaded into the canoe. Later, a claim for £5-0-0 was submitted to cover the cost of repair. The claim was passed to the Qtr. Master, Southern Command, Collins Barracks. The Department of Finance settled the claim in full. (Reference G.2/X/0922). Sgt. Fox was buried in the Church of Ireland Cemetery, Miltown Malbay, Co. Clare, at 4:30pm on January 29th 1942. (Reference G.2/X/0922)

A large crowd attended the funeral that afternoon. During the burial service, a man in the crowd pushed his way to the front, and handed some photographs to one of the NCOs on duty, saying *"Take these, they might haunt me"*, then melted into the crowd. The man was not identified. The photographs most likely related to the crew, and were picked up by the man along the shore, because in the days following the crash, some private documents were washed ashore on the tide and scattered by the wind. Many were badly damaged, but some were identified by the pilot as members of his crew, and others as members of 201 Squadron. (Reference S.1 /85, Dated Feb. 13th 1942)

After discharge from Mallow Military Hospital, on December 10^{th,} Flight Lt. Fleming reported the loss of his RAF Great coat and cap, which were in the aircraft. The clothing was not found in the wreckage after it drifted ashore. Captain Daly confirmed this in his reply to Fleming, on January 5th 1942. (Reference 13SQ/S/Misc). All other personal effects were returned to him at the Curragh Detention Centre, on Dec.10th 1941. (Reference S.41/108). On the11th Dec., Flight Lt. Fleming wrote to Miss Bette Parrott, 4 Holybank, Muswell Hill, London N10, England. (Reference S.41/108, letter dated Dec.11th 1941).

Following release from Mallow Military Hospital, Sgt. James C.

Masterson joined his pilot at the Curragh Detention Centre on Dec.17th. (Non-reference letter of Dec.17th 1941)

In later years, Jim often related that on discovering the rubber dinghy was unusable, he discarded his uniform because he knew it would weigh him down as it became saturated. The military archive material fully supports his story, with the record of a clothing issue to him of a suit, overcoat, vest, shirt, collar, tie, socks and boots; because he arrived without clothing is the stated reason for the issue. (Reference Q.5 /41).

Following the detention of the two aviators, the historical file suggests they were quickly in contact with their families and friends, because by the end of January 1942, Fleming had received 15 letters, and Masterson 19, including one batch of 7 on Christmas Eve. From other published accounts, it appears the U.K. Representative to Eire made sure they were well looked after in terms of food and beverage. Rationing of that era did not appear to have any impact on their supplies, and on making them comfortable at the Curragh.

Life was not bad for the internees at the Curragh, but Flight Lt. Fleming and fellow Canadian Pilot Officer Bobby Keefer, longed to get back to active service, and on August 17th 1942, they escaped custody and safely reached N. Ireland. After a period of leave, Fleming got his wish, and returned to flying duties. He was assigned to Ferry Command in January 1943, where he served until September 1943, when he was promoted to Squadron Leader.

Following promotion he was assigned to Fighter Command. No record of his flying activities with Fighter Command was traced, but Squadron Leader (Pilot) J.G. Fleming was reported missing in action over Europe on September 6th 1944. The death of Squadron Leader (Pilot) J.G. Fleming was confirmed in AFRO 1085/45 dated June 29th 1945. He was laid to rest in Rheinberg War Cemetery, Germany.

Other interesting documents, from the archive file, are reproduced as reprinted copied below. They are difficult to include as photocopies, due to their quality, but are true copies of the originals. The first document is from the U.K. Representative to Eire, expressing his thanks to Oscar Traynor, T.D., for the organisation and efficiency, with which the funerals of the victims were handled. It's an interesting example of the very good relationships that existed throughout the war between Eire and the U.K., and completely contrary to the Black Malicious Propaganda one reads of in the popular press.

United Kingdom Representative to Eire
50 Upper Mount Street,
Dublin.
16th December 1941

Dear Mr. Traynor,

Mr. Lynwood, my attaché, attended the recent funeral of the British airmen who were drowned off Doonbeg last week, and I once again have to thank you for the courtesy, sympathy and efficiency with which the funeral arrangements were carried out.

Would you be good enough to convey my thanks to the Chief of Staff for his actions in sending a representative, and to those concerned for the kindness and consideration shown on this sad occasion?

Yours sincerely,
Signed; J. Maffey.

O. Traynor, Esq. T.D.

HEADQUARTERS,
13th Cyclist Squadron, Military Post,
Kilrush,
Co. Clare.
20th December 1941

Captain O'Brien,
Officer I/C Message Centre;
G2 Branch, Sarsfield Barracks,
Limerick.

Sir,
I have the honour to inform you of a number of facts in connection with the crash of the British Sea-Plane "Pluto", on Doughmore Strand, Co. Clare, on the night of the 3rd December 1941, and which, in my estimate, are worthy of the highest praise.

1) Messrs Simon McCarthy, Michael Stack and Michael Stack (junior), of Coolmore, Doonbeg, rescued Flight Lieut. Fleming, whom they observed struggling in the rough sea. At great risk to their own lives, they entered the water and brought him safely ashore to the house of Mr. Stack. It was their quick activity and resourcefulness that was responsible for saving the life of Flight Lieut. Fleming.

2) Michael O'Donovan of Cloonmore, reported to me that the 'plane had crashed at Doughmore, and that two men had been brought ashore. He cycled five miles to carry this information to me. It was his initiative that resulted in my getting to the scene of the crash before the civilian population arrived, and so we were able to keep unauthorised persons from interfering with the wreckage.

3) Patrick Shanahan, Carrowmore, North, Doonbeg, found Sgt. Masterson, R.A.F. outside the window of his residence. He brought him into the house and gave him every attention and care possible. This man, Patrick Shanahan, had a brother killed by the Black and Tans during the "Troubles" in Ireland, and still had no ill feeling against this British Airman and gave him everything possible to make him comfortable.

In view of the above facts, I would like if it were possible, to thank the personnel publicly, because I am sure that their acts were heroic and noteworthy. Besides these people would appreciate a word of praise and thanks from the Army Authorities, and it would also encourage the civilian population to still greater co-operation should the occasion arise in the future.

I have the honour to be Sir,
Your Obedient Servant,
Signed: D.D. Spicer 2nd Lieut. For Captain P. Daly (V.F)
Officer Commanding 13th Cyclist Squadron, Cavalry Corps. Kilrush

The Royal Humane Society acknowledged the heroic efforts of Simon McCarthy, Michael Stack and Michael Stack (Jnr), with Parchment Certificates for saving the life of Flight Lt. James Grant Fleming, on the evening of December 3rd 1941.

Michael O'Donovan's contribution was recognised by the Irish Army, and Patrick Shanahan was also awarded the RHS Parchment Certificate, for attempting to save an air man who had drowned in the sea.

There is no record in the archives that identifies who was responsible for the citation sent to the Royal Humane Society. Eire was neutral, so military correspondence of this nature was unlikely, but there is a strong possibility that it was Canon and Lady Elliott, the Church of Ireland Presbytery, Milltown Malbay, Co. Clare.

One little known fact about Sunderland W3988, is that in no other Flying Boat crash after W3988, were the survivors interned in Eire. In all subsequent crashes, de Valera decided that Flying Boat air crews should be treated as distressed mariners, and allowed to leave the country. This only applied to Allied crews, and for all subsequent crashes the survivors and any bodies recovered were taken to the border at Belleek, by the Irish Army and handed over to the RAF with full military honours. As a young lad, I was present on a few occasions for the ceremonies. Where we lived was just a few hundred yards from the border, and if anything unusual happened, I could see it. There are 80 war graves in Irvinestown, Co. Fermanagh, which is close to Castle Archdale, where about 360 men, who served on Lough Erne, lost their lives during the war. Many of the RAF airmen's bodies were returned to their families in Britain. A good number went down with their planes in the Atlantic and have no known graves. A list of them is included in another chapter.

My family roots can be traced to Co. Clare, when an O'Loughlin came to Fermanagh as a hedge school master. The Rev. Canon Elliott was a native of Belleek, and I often seen him on visits home. He was known as 'Crab Elliott' in Miltown Malbay. He acquired the name as he was an excellent swimmer, and he would don an old suit and dive into the sea only to reappear with the pockets of the suit full of crabs.

The story of Sunderland W3988 did not end in 1941, but rather in October 1991, 50 years after the loss of the Flying Boat. Barrie and Pauline Hardesty from Norfolk, England, made a visit to Doonbeg, to see the graves of the airmen. The Hardesty's were interested in war graves, and collected data for sharing with relatives unable to travel. They had heard of the RAF graves, and made enquiries around Doonbeg. They were directed to Tom O'Gorman, a local schoolteacher, who told them the story of the crash. They also met with Patrick Shanahan, and took photographs of the old Shanahan house, and the rocky approach that Jim Masterson had to negotiate to reach safety. In a letter to Tom, they said that Jim Masterson lived just 20 miles from them, and they had visited them after their trip to Ireland. Jim gave them a detailed account of the crash and his rescue. Barrie also wrote to Patrick Shanahan, thanking him for all the help he had given, and how they had the pleasure of meeting Jim and his wife on their return.

Jim Masterson wrote to Patrick after he had met with the Hardesty's, and thanked Patrick for the ½ bottle of Irish whiskey he had sent over with them. Jim said that the whiskey would be opened on 3rd December, when, with members of their family, they would mark the anniversary of the crash. Jim promised to make the trip back to Doonbeg in the near future.

In 1991, Barrie Hardesty wrote to the editor of the Clare Champion, asking if he had a report of the crash in their paper in 1941.There was strict press censorship during the war years, because the de Valera government did not want the world to know that most RAF crews forced to land in Eire, were quietly allowed to travel to N. Ireland, and return to active service. Barrie and Pauline Hardesty were known as regular visitors to Ireland, and a friend asked them to try and find the grave of his brother, who had died in a crash and was buried in Miltown Malbay, Co. Clare. They did locate the grave of LAC Frederick Lea, and took photographs of it for his brother.

Jim Masterson made a return visit to Doonbeg at the end of September 1993, and renewed his friendship with Patrick Shanahan. In February 1992, Patrick had a letter from a Joyce Allsworth, nee Reed. Joyce had asked a friend of hers from Tralee if she could find out anything about the crash of a Sunderland somewhere on the West Coast of Ireland. Her boyfriend, Sgt. Sidney Epps, had died in the crash, and was buried in Co. Clare. Later on in February, Patrick wrote to Barrie Hardesty, and told him that he had received a letter from Joyce, which he replied to, giving all the details he remembered. He also took photographs of the grave, and sent them to Joyce. He said she had sent him a lovely letter, and he had great sympathy for her.

Patrick Shanahan died in February 2000, aged 91 years, and when Jim Masterson died in 1994, his family brought his ashes to Doughmore and scattered them on the shore. The courage and caring of the people of Co. Clare was typical of Irish people during the war. They overlooked the many years of conflict that had existed when the country was ruled by England. Their thoughts about the young airmen who died was that "They were some mothers sons", and were treated with respect and dignity.

The chapter closed with the death of Jim Masterson. The crash of Sunderland W3988 cost nine young lives, another story of the horrors of war. It is highly probable that the entire crew would have survived, were it not for the loss of the port engine at time of landing. The big Pegasus MK. XV111 engine hit a submerged rock, and to the present day sits on that rocky shelf. On occasions like a March spring tide, the outline of the engine is clearly visible above the water. Today, it is covered in marine growth, but older local people are able to point to it from the Doughmore Strand.

It is quite awesome to stand there on the shore at low tide, especially a spring tide, and see how close to safety that unfortunate crew was. Just a few meters further north and Pluto would have missed the rocky shelf. This would have given the craft an excellent chance of gliding safely along the sandy beach, before coming to a halt in shallow waters.

It would not have been possible to compile the story of Sunderland W3988 without the help of a number of people from Doonbeg. Their choice was not to have their names mentioned. They know who they are and their help is greatly appreciated.

CHAPTER 5

Sunderland W4036 and the Dolphin family

On Thursday 18th November 1943, Castle Archdale based Sunderland W4036, of 201 Squadron, was engaged in a local flying exercise on Lough Erne. Two new pilots were being trained on take-offs and landings (known as circuits and bumps), on the lake. On the final landing, the port wing of the plane hit the water, and the Sunderland crashed into the lake. Killed in the accident was Sgt. Elvet Parry, R.A.F,. a 20 year old crew member from Flintshire, Wales. Missing were F/Lt. Douglas James Dolphin, a 23 year old pilot from Canada, and Sgt. John Bosanko Green, R.A.F. Wireless Operator, aged 23. The bodies of the two missing men were never recovered, and are still on the wreck of the Sunderland on the bed of the lake. It is one of two recognised war graves in Lough Erne.

Injured were F/O Maurice Alexander, R.A.F., Pilot; Sgt. John B. Cummings, R.A.F.; A/G. Sgt. Clement Vernon Ford, R.A.F., F/Eng.; F/O Douglas Harry Longland, R.A.F., Pilot; and F.O. Thomas H. Gleig, R.C.A.F.

During such exercises, a pinnace boat was always in attendance, and it picked up the body of Sgt. Parry and the survivors from the water. The sad news of the deaths of the young airmen, was conveyed to their families. In Toronto, Canada, it was received by June, the wife of Douglas Dolphin. They had been married shortly before he left for England. Also to get the dreaded news was his father, Charles B. Dolphin, his mother Doris, and the other members of the Dolphin family. In May 1946, Mr. Charles Dolphin made the long journey to Ireland, to visit the place where his son had died, and where his body was still in the wreckage of the Sunderland, on the bed of Lough Erne. He had a hope that the wreckage might be located, his son's body recovered, and brought back to Canada. With Castle Archdale being still operational, Charles received full co-operation from the Royal Air Force officers there, and from the diving team who operated on the lake as well as local people.

Realising that there was no hope of locating the Sunderland, Mr. Dolphin, with the help of the Commanding Officer, made plans to have a memorial service out on the lake, as close as possible to where the plane had crashed. The service was not only to honour Douglas Dolphin, but also the 17 other men whose bodies rested in the lake. The Rector of the local Church of Ireland, Rev. John Switzer, was pleased to conduct the service.

Mr. Wm. D. Morrow, a reporter from a leading Belfast newspaper, was sent to cover the event. Naturally, Mr. Dolphin was very busy on the day, and for some time after. Wm. Morrow sent a letter to the family in Toronto, describing the ceremony. It was addressed to Douglas's two sisters, and brother Bob.

"I was sent down by my paper to report the beautiful memorial service on the Lake, and as your Dad had so much to attend to, I thought I would drop you a note. He had said to me on Sunday, "How much my two girls would have loved to have been here today". I am sure you were with us in spirit, as we stood on the deck of the barge, and took part in the ceremony. Your dear Dad looked so charming and kindly, and at the same time pathetic, as he moved down the steps to cast the Maple Cross into the water. It has been my duty to report on many ceremonies, but none so touching as this one. The lake lay peaceful and still for miles. Birds stirred occasionally in the thick woods all around, and the water looked like a great sheet of glass stretching away for miles. Everyone was so reverent and still, as if they were conscious of some great loss. We went out by fast motor launch, and I helped to carry the flowers to the barge. It seemed, as we stood in the stillness, that the gallant lads were very near to us all. Somewhere in the dark waters they slept on, undisturbed by war and strife, their duty over, and the last Great Flight completed. Amongst the large number of people on the barge, were the Commanding Officer and staff of the R.A.F., a firing party, a bugler to sound the Last Post, and the Rev. John Switzer. A representative of the Air Ministry, newspaper reporters, and roughly clad farm workers, fishermen and salvage men, lined up on the deck, all to pay tribute. The sacrifice of the 18 who sleep in the lake was not in vain. Death has closed around them, but their noble sacrifice will not be forgotten. Your Dad was very brave throughout, and was most reverent and dignified in every thing that he arranged. We were all

moved as he stood on the edge of the little platform, and repeated a few words of farewell to your dear brother".

The altar on the barge was draped with a Canadian flag, which once flew at the gate of the Dolphin home in Toronto.

There are no roses on this airman's grave,
No Lilies on the Broad Lough wave.
The only tribute is the mute swans sweeps,
And the tear drop that a sweetheart weeps!

During his time here in Fermanagh, Charles sent regular letters home to his wife and family, telling them all about the events. On the evening after the ceremony, Mr. Dolphin was sitting in his hotel room writing to his wife Doris. *"I am looking right up the lake, and the sun is setting in the west, shinning on you and on me at the same time, but most marvellous of all, it is setting exactly over the area in the lake where Doug lies, and the lake at that spot is shinning gold. I do not believe that these things are just co-incidence. Only God alone could line up all these things, and I am grateful to Him. It is inspiring, and I take it as a message of faith from our Creator and our boy".* Before leaving for home, Charles Dolphin expressed the wish that some day a suitable memorial would be put in place in honour of his son and his comrades. (Now this has been done.)

In 2003 another event related to Douglas Dolphin took place. The Churchill and Tully Castle Historical Society had, for some time, being considering marking the crash of a Catalina in their district. In the early hours of the morning of 20th November 1944, Catalina JX 242, was returning from an Atlantic patrol when it crashed on the Barr of Wealt Mountain, with the loss of 8 crew members. Two men survived the crash. With the permission of the Forestry Department, a memorial stone with the names of the dead men was placed at Lough Navar view point. This place overlooked Lough Erne, and is visited ever year by large numbers of people, to enjoy the beautiful scenery. The society also decided to place a matching memorial stone at the View Point, in honour of Douglas Dolphin, his comrades from Sunderland W4036, and all the young air men who had died while serving on Lough Erne. The unveiling ceremony, arranged by the members of the Historical Society, who were assisted by local historians Breege McCusker and Joe O'Loughlin, is described in detail in the book "Voices of the Donegal

Corridor". As no one at that time had any contact details for the Dolphin family, they were unaware of the ceremony. The event, which was attended by about 400 guests, got full coverage in the papers, radio and television. It was also reported in detail, by aviation journals in England.

We now move ahead to the year 2006, when an American film research team came to Fermanagh, to investigate the possibility of locating any Catalina Flying Boats that were reputed to have been scuttled in the lake after the war. The team asked me to assist them with any information I had, and to guide them during the project. A team of deep diving experts from England, led by Steve Carmichael–Timson (a notable wreck diver from Wales), were hired by the film crew to search the lake. Nothing positive was found by the dive team that either the film crew or myself was made aware of. Since then, members of the film crew including Teri Knapp have kept in contact with me.

The following year, 2007, Bob Dolphin, brother of Douglas, received a phone call in his home in Canada, at 9pm on a Saturday evening in May. The caller identified himself as Steve Carmichael-Timson, who claimed that after a year of searching, he had discovered the wreck of Sunderland W4036. Bob was naturally quite shocked by this news, and thought it was a prank. The diver gave him several precise details about Douglas, that he must have obtained by researching Canadian air force records, as they were not known to anyone over there. Bob Dolphin, and his sister Shirley Brangers, communicated regularly with Carmichael-Timson, and plans were made for the family to come to Fermanagh, and attend to a memorial service to be held on Lough Erne, on 29th September, over the spot where the diver had claimed to have located the Sunderland. Bob was accompanied by his wife Ruth, his sister Shirley, granddaughter Jennifer Dolphin, and other family members. Bob said words cannot describe how he felt coming to the place where his brother had died. The ceremony was filmed by Will Davies of Solo Television from Wales, which was given exclusive access by the diving team involved in locating the plane. Bob said it was rather tiring being interviewed by the film crew, but nevertheless, he said it was a beautiful event, presided over by the Chaplain of the Royal Air Force, The Rev. Derek Weir. The haunting sounds of the Bugler's rendition of the Last Post floated out across the water, as he and his family stood on the Mahoo jetty, on the shore of the lake. The bugler was Andrew Gordon, a member of the Churchill Silver Band. Young Andrew had sounded the Last Post at a number of similar memorial services. Bob was particularly struck by the presence of two young

R.A.F. Flight Lieutenants, who were so like his brother. Following the memorial ceremony, the families of the three fallen airmen were taken out to the crash site, to place wreaths on the water's surface, above where the Sunderland lies on the bed of the lake. The ceremony was filmed by Paul Clark of Ulster Tele-Vision, and featured in the news that evening. It was also the lead story in the local newspapers. The story was given extensive coverage in the Canadian magazine "Muskoka", after an interview with Bob Dolphin.

The ceremony was attended by many local people, including the members of the Churchill and Tully Castle Historical Society. From them, the Dolphin family learned for the first time about the memorial stone in honour of Douglas and his comrades at the Lough Navar View Point. Unfortunately, the time schedule did not give them the opportunity to see the stone. Also at the ceremony, were Ida Parry/Mould and Mary Garston from North Wales, sisters of Sgt. Parry, and Aine Hind from England, sister of Sgt. Green. Sadly the diver, Steve Carmichael-Timson, was to die tragically on Sunday, 2nd March 2008.

Breege McCusker and I were at the ceremony, and I presented the families with copies of the Donegal Corridor book. As I did not have enough copies with me for them all, I posted more out to the Dolphin family in Canada, and so was established a wonderful friendship with the family. I had some lovely letters of appreciation from them, particularly from Bob, who sent me copies of letters describing the visit of his father to Ireland in 1946, and the magazine story of their own visit in 2007. He was so happy to meet many Fermanagh people at the ceremony, and to learn about the memorial stone. He knew that the spirit of his brother, Douglas, was secure in the hearts of many fine people around the shores of Lough Erne. Bob phoned me early in 2010, and we had a lovely conversation. He was so proud of the family connection with Ireland that he wished to use the Irish version 'Seamus' of James. Sadly, Bob/Seamus passed away on the 27th May 2010, just a few months afterwards.

After the loss of Sunderland W4036, nothing was heard about F/O T.H. Gleig. Apparently he was not seriously injured, and returned to flying duties shortly after. Then, on 24th Nov. 1945, he wrote to Charlie and Doris Dolphin. Shirley Brangers, Doug's sister, sent me a copy of the letter.

Mr. T. H. Glieg, Ex F/L . R.C.A.F.
Box 544
Chilliwack. B.C.
Nov. 24th /45.

C.B. Dolphin,
43 Victoria St., Toronto, Ontario, Canada.

Dear Mr. Dolphin,
It is strange that I should hear from you today. Last night I had a dream, and in it, I was looking over Doug's Scrap book and Snap album again. I saw his snap's image taken at Elementary and Service flying school, the Middle East and Castle Archdale. I recall in the dream how much I wished I had kept such a collection of mementos. The reason I did not was due to the feeling I had throughout my service career overseas, that I might not return and I would thus avoid a collection being received by my wife and son.

Yes! Mr. Dolphin, I was a member of Doug's crew from O.T.U. in Scotland right up until the night of his death. I learned to know him as a fine big youngster with the keenest of blue eyes. Good at billiards and snooker and especially good at push penny. A game I used to play quite often with him in the Mess. I could never beat him.

As a captain he was superb. Fully confident and capable and one who gained the respect and admiration of all the members of his crew. His flying was perfect and his knowledge of all phases of aircrew trades, extraordinary. Night landings were just as routine as day landings with Doug at the controls. Never a bump or a bounce, we were always water borne before we knew it. Just prior to our accident we had been grounded for a week or so due to maintenance on our own aircraft. Then the inevitable circuit and bumps by night program came out with our names on it. It called for F/L Dolphin and skeleton crew of five. Doug was to give instructions to two junior Captain Pilots in the take-off and landing.

Doug asked me to be one of the five crew members and I was proud that he thought my services were necessary. We were not familiar with the other two pilots; they had just arrived on the Squadron from the O.T.U. The other crew members besides, Doug and myself, were Elvet Parry, air gunner, Taffy Ford and Bill Cummings, 1st and second engineers, Johnny Green and myself, W.A.G. The Lough was glassy calm which makes for a good landing.

Doug did the first couple of circuits and each time his take-off and landing was perfect.

He then instructed one of the other Pilots to take over whilst he sat in the second Pilots seat. My position was on the wireless seat, except before take offs and landings, when I would flash the pinnace in charge of the flight path by Aidis lamp to get permission to land. A blackout curtain separated my position from that of the Pilots, so that I did not see either Doug or the other two Pilots after the take-off. Green and Parry stayed below deck in the ward room after the initial take-off. The other Pilot took off O.K. and I could hear Doug giving him instructions in landing technique over the intercom during our approach to land. The pilot seemed to be coming in left wing low and I remember I looked out the Astra dome and saw the first flare path light disappearing under our wing. Doug told him to gun the throttle and pull her up and once again we made the circuit only to follow the same procedure. The third time we seemed to be coming in nice and level. I could see the visual horizon from the Astra dome, when up came the nose and then down with a crash. It all happened so sudden I don't think any of us knew just what was happening, except the Pilot flying the air craft. No word was spoken over the intercom. I found myself flat on my back on the deck being crushed between the wireless and navigators tables. The water came in fast and I could see my way out through the Astra dome above my head of the metal would soon release me. I prayed like I'd never prayed before. Then all of a sudden I found myself free and able to fight the Astra dome catches off and remove the dome. I slid right into the water followed by the two engineers. The other two pilots escaped through the pilot's window just as the aircraft disappeared 45 seconds after the crash. I looked around for Doug and the other boy's, Johnny and Dave (Elvet) but could not see them and right up until the dinghy picked us up I kept expecting to see their heads come popping to the surface.

Reluctantly we were taken away for the shore leaving the pinnace and its crew to continue the search. Somehow I think that Doug was either knocked unconscious or attempted to get back to myself and the other boys. Knowing Doug, I know that his own safety would be his last thought. It was just like loosing a brother to loose Doug and my deepest sympathy go out to Mrs. Dolphin and yourself, as well as his lovely wife. He loved you all so much and outside of the above I have little to add. I suffered only a fractured nose and badly bruised ribs and arm. I recovered back to flying health within six weeks. I did not write you Mr. Dolphin because I just didn't know where to start and Glen Ferguson our regular 2nd Pilot said he would write. I trust that this will help you in your determined effort to find Doug's body and that you get the satisfaction and peace of mind from your trip to Castle Archdale this summer.

God Bless you,

Yours sincerely, Tommy Glieg

CHAPTER 6

Norm Muffitt and the fate of Catalina FP120

The story of how Ted Muffitt's Catalina was lost without trace in the Atlantic Ocean is documented in my Donegal Corridor book. Norm Muffitt, Ted's son, was introduced to me by my friends Les and Maureen Ingram, who live in Scotland. Since Norm contacted me in February 2004, we built up a wonderful friendship which lasted until Norm sadly passed away in 2011, after a short illness. Over the years, we corresponded regularly, and discovered many of the comrades who had served with Ted at Killadeas, with 131 Operational Training Unit. A comrade of Norm's, Joe Collinson, and his wife Agnes, made a surprise visit to Belleek, in June 2007. Joe and Norm were both retired Mounties. They also had a great interest in motor bikes, and belonged to the local bike club. Together with their wives, they went on many enjoyable outings. Shortly after Joe and Agnes returned to Canada, he visited the Nanton Air Museum, where he saw a plaque for a Clarence Loree Scott, who died in the Halifax LK 704 crash at Bundoran, on the 23rd January 1944. Joe was aware from my Donegal book of the story of this crash. Joe has kept in touch with me ever since, and during Norm's final illness he gave me all the news and an account of Norm's funeral.

This is an account given in a book 'The Kid Glove Pilot' by Allan Deller, a comrade of Ted's, of the training done by Ted Muffitt and his comrades, who were based on Lough Erne, Co. Fermanagh, N. Ireland.

The flying on this conversion course involved the usual 'circuits and bumps', (landing and takeoff's) day and night, navigation exercises, air-firing and low-level practice bombing (at 50 feet). We also did several very useful Operational Flying Exercises (OFE's) which simulated actual operations –

briefing, over-ocean flight and debriefing and included dropping two live depth charges. We were instructed to send a wireless code word just before we dropped the DC's and on one of these sorties the signal was sent and the aircraft then disappeared and was never seen again. It was obviously vital to try to sort out the mystery so one of the most experienced pilots on the course, a really splendid Canadian, Ted Muffitt, who had been a bush pilot in the far north of Canada, was sent out accompanied by a second aircraft; the required signal was sent and next second the crew in the companion aircraft were transfixed with horror to see the depth charges explode on the surface 50 feet directly below Ted's aircraft which disintegrated with the huge power of the Torpex explosive and disappeared in seconds without trace. Painstaking checking and research subsequently showed that our DC's had been fitted with faulty 'pistol's which caused the charge to explode on impact instead of setting off at 25 feet depth where the water pressure would trigger it. A brave and fearless man gave his life to ensure that others did not suffer a sad death caused by the mistakes of others.

It was quite by chance that I acquired the book 'The Kid Glove Pilot' by Allan Deller. He got the title from the fact that when flying, he always wore a pair of kid leather gloves. The book was advertised by a publisher, and when I saw that it was about Flying Boats, I had to buy it, little realising how important it would become. When I reached the chapter about Ted Muffitt, I immediately e-mailed that section to Norm in Canada. This is the reply I got right away on 19th September 2004.

Joe,
I cannot begin to tell you how much your e-mail has meant to all of us over here. When I tried to read the message to my mother, I found myself choking up. It has indeed been a revelation. Considering the author is probably recalling things from old notes or memories, he was pretty accurate. The spelling of the last name was close, and his reference to Dad being a bush pilot in the north was obviously a twist on Dad's service in the Artic with the RCMP. It was there that he learned to navigate by the stars etc.
His description of my Dad was very kind, and my mother was deeply touched. She told me that many years ago, they had heard something about Depth Charges causing the loss of the Catalina, but had discounted it as there appeared to be no supporting data. We always just assumed that he had gone

out on that day alone. Joe, I cannot begin to tell you how happy you have made our whole family. Bless you for your assistance and your caring. To get the true story does give me a feeling of closeness to the father I never really knew. I will get back to you soon. Norm.

Another letter I got on 19th September 2004 from Jen Jones.

Hello,

My name is Jennifer Jones; I am Norm Muffitt's daughter, and granddaughter of Ted Muffitt. My Dad forwarded the photos you sent him of the flowers you placed at the marker, and the letter you placed there on our behalf. I just wanted to say thank you for doing this. I've spoken to my father, and I know it has meant a lot to him as well, and renewed a connection to his father's memory. Your thoughtfulness is much appreciated.

Jen Jones.

I replied to this e-mail right away, and on 20th September I had this message from Jen.

Joe,

Thanks for your e-mail and it is so nice to get to know you. I can't tell you how much your research into the Catalina pilots and history of the area from World War 2 has meant, especially to my Dad. As you know, he was left alone with his Mum and infant sister, Monda, as a toddler when his Dad passed away, and for all those years they had no information re; his death, other than his plane failed to return from a mission.

I know it has given him an enormous relief and some closure to hear these details, and certainly renewed the sense of pride he always felt about his Dad, now knowing that he did not die from any fault of his own, or for a futile reason. My husband Stewart's mother is from Sligo, and soon we plan to come to Ireland on a visit when we will meet you.

Cheers from Jen.

I had already sent to Norm and his family copies of my Donegal Corridor book, and I arranged to have copies of the 'Kid Glove Pilot' sent to his mother, Hester, and his sister, Monda Ellis.

As a tribute to his father, Norm Muffitt compiled this article for the Royal Canadian Mounted Police journal. **"The Quarterly".**

THE SEARCH

Ex Cst. E.E. (Ted) Muffitt, Reg. No. 11892, departed Killadeas RAF Coastal Command Seaplane base in Northern Ireland, as the Captain of Catalina FP120, on 2nd November 1943. Ted failed to return, and he and his entire crew disappeared somewhere over the Atlantic Ocean.

Ted's wife, Hester, received a short telegram advising her that "F/L E.E. Muffitt was missing and believed killed, on 2nd November 1943", and she was left alone to raise their infant children, Norman, 17 months, and Monda, 5 months old. How and why Ted's aircraft disappeared without a trace has haunted the Muffitt family for over 60 years.

Ted's son, 21711 ex S/Sgt. Norm Muffitt, served in Air Service as a pilot with the force and spent many hours researching the death of his father. It was in 2003 that he stumbled upon a very unusual group of individuals, led by historian and author Joe O'Loughlin, of Belleek in Northern Ireland.

Joe's group researched Coastal Command Records from the Lough Erne area, searching out and marking crash sites, and erecting small monuments to the lost Coastal Command crews. The research and monuments are financed through the generosity of the group members themselves. A number of Canadian families have received information on how their loved ones perished during the war, along with photos and information on where and how they lived during that turbulent time, from this dedicated group. Some of these families have even travelled to Northern Ireland and the old base at 131 OTU RAF Station, at Killadeas. Here they meet Joe O'Loughlin, and his group composed of wartime historians Breege McCusker, James Stewart and Les Ingram, who are dedicated to helping them find closure after these many years.

Even with Joe's able assistance the facts surrounding the loss of Catalina FP120, and ex Cst. Ted Muffitt, remained a mystery until one day, in 2004, Norman received an e-mail from Ireland. Joe and his group had stumbled upon a recently published book titled *"The Kid Glove Pilot"*, written by a wartime Coastal Command Pilot named Allan Deller. Deller had served with Ted Muffitt during the war, and described in detail how Ted and his crew met their untimely end. Deller wrote that Muffitt, and another Canadian Crew, were asked to do the same mission pattern as a Catalina that had gone missing on a previous patrol. The missing Catalina had wired their base that they were dropping depth charges on a routine training exercise. They were never heard of again, and no trace was ever found of the missing aircraft and crew.

F/L Muffitt and his crew descended to fifty feet above the ocean while a second Catalina observed from a safe altitude, and there they released their depth charges. A depth charge which is dropped from this very low altitude, is designed to sink to a depth of twenty five feet before exploding with sufficient force to rupture the steel hull of a German Submarine. In this case however, the depth charges exploded on contact with the sea directly beneath the aluminium skinned Catalina. The aircraft and crew were instantly destroyed. During a telephone exchange, Deller spoke to the Muffitt family in glowing terms of Ted's character, and how his service in the RCMP had helped him as a wartime pilot. He also revealed that the premature explosion was caused by a design fault in the depth charge fuse, and as a direct result of this accident, the fault was able to be corrected, saving other crews a similar fate.

Ted's wife, Hester, died in 2007, but before her death she learned the details of her husband's last flight, and said that this knowledge had brought her peace, and provided the closure she had sought for these many years.

There was an interesting sideline to this investigation when Norman discovered that his father's loss had also been recorded in a book written by an Australian, ex Squadron Leader Bruce Daymond, DSO/DFC. Mr. Daymond's diaries were published under the title, "An Innocent Abroad – of Submarines and Spies", and in this book, he describes how he, Ted, and Ted's Canadian Co-Pilot, Doug Disney, had gone to Dublin on leave, where they rented some horses for an afternoon ride. He remarked that Ted's mount was very spirited, but met his match, as Ted had been a member of the RCMP Musical Ride before the war. He also talked of that terrible day in November of 1943, and the impact Ted's loss had on his comrades.

Norman's daughter, Jennifer, is a member of the Hamilton City Police, and married to a retired police office, currently serving in the Canadian Army. In June 2009, Jennifer, husband, Stewart Jones, and son, Ryan, travelled to Northern Ireland and paid a visit to the old seaplane base on Lough Erne.

Learning of the Jones family arrival, Joe O'Loughlin ordered a wreath shaped as an RCAF Roundel, and rounded up a Canadian Flag. Killadeas today is the site of the Lough Erne Yacht Club, and Joe arranged with Yacht Club Chairman, Michael Clarke, and Commodore Mary Anne Sutton, to host a wreath laying ceremony at the OUT Squadron Memorial. On the big day, Jennifer Jones, accompanied by Stewart and Ryan, laid the wreath for her late Grandfather, and gave a short speech, where she thanked the wonderful people of Ireland who's passion it is to ensure the Coastal Command aircrews who perished on wartime operations, are not forgotten.

Norman and his family have been in touch with both authors, and received a photo from Bruce Daymond, just before his death in 2008, showing the participants of No 7 Captains course, at Killadeas in 1943. In the front row one sees Ted Muffitt sitting beside authors, Bruce Daymand and Allan Deller.

Joe O'Loughlin authored a book titled "Voices of the Donegal Corridor" wherein he includes a chapter describing the family's search for information on Ted Muffitt. The front cover has a photo of Ted and his mates, and there are a number of family photos illustrating the story of the Muffitt family search. The book is a "must read" for any serious student of World War Two.

Patience, and the good will of others, have paid huge dividends. Ex Cst. E.E. (Ted) Muffitt can now rest in peace, and this investigation will be considered "Concluded here".

Ex 21711 S/Sgt. N.C. Muffitt (Retired) August 2009.

Words of appreciation by Jennifer Jones at the wreath laying, Killadeas

Commodore Mary Anne, Chairman Michael Clarke, and all of my new found friends, who have assembled here on the shores of Lough Erne, I am deeply moved that so many people should be present here for this special occasion. My husband, Stewart, Ryan and I anticipated a quiet wreath laying ceremony here at Killadeas, a place that held so many good memories for my Grandfather, Ted Muffitt. It is mainly due to the organising ability of Michael Clarke, that such a suitable ceremony has been planned. For that Michael, I thank you from my heart.

For most of my life, the loss of my Grandfather, Ted, has been shrouded in mystery. We had no idea of how he lost his life. We wondered if he had suffered when his plane was lost, or if by some

chance, he, as pilot, made a mistake that resulted in the loss of Catalina FP120 and it's crew. All sorts of things went through the minds of my dear Grandmother, and my Dad, Norm, as he grew up. I think Dad's first contact on this side of the Atlantic Ocean, about 7 years ago, was with Les Ingram, who lives in Scotland. Les's wife, Maureen, lost her Dad, Guy Wilkinson, in the crash of a Sunderland, in the South of Ireland, in 1943. Guy is buried in the war graves in Irvinestown. Les led my Dad to Joe O'Loughlin, James Stewart, Breege McCusker and others. Suddenly, the Irish mists of time were swept away, and we as a family learned all the facts of how Ted lost his life.

Words cannot adequately explain what this meant to our family, especially to my Grandmother, Hester, my Dad, and my Aunt Monda. Thankfully, Grand mother lived long enough to learn what happened, and was alert enough to appreciate it all. Over hundreds of years, there has been a strong connection between my homeland, Canada, and this Green Island of Ireland. I am so proud of my husband's family Irish roots, and for us to be here today is an experience of a lifetime.

On behalf of all our family, I thank you for being present here today to pay tribute, not only to Ted Muffitt, but also to all the other airmen who served here during World War

My gratitude to Michael Clarke, who at very short notice, made the plans for the Lough Erne Yacht Club to host this moving ceremony.

Jennifer, Stewart, and Ryan, had thought to place a wreath quietly on the shores of Lough Erne at Killadeas, in memory of her Grandfather, Fl/Lt. Edward Earle Muffitt, known to his friends as Ted. Once Michael Clarke was made aware of the family coming to Fermanagh, he organised this moving and dignified ceremony, as a tribute, not only to Ted, but also to the some 360 airmen who lost their lives while serving on Lough Erne.

For the duration of the ceremony, the Yacht Club flag was lowered from the flag pole, and the Canadian Air Force Flag hoisted in its place. The Commodore, Mary Anne Sutton, treated all present to tea and other suitable refreshments.

In Canada at the time, the local paper in the obituary to Ted said, "Muffitt, Edward Earle, Fl./Lt. of Coe Hill Ontario. Killed, aged 34".

Sometime after Jennifer and her family returned to Canada, they sent me, as a token of appreciation, a lovely cast scale model of a Catalina. Naturally it is one of my most treasured possessions.

Sadly, Norm Muffitt died on Friday, 19th August 2011, from tumours of the brain. He had told me in our correspondence about the state of his health. I was naturally saddened, and at the same time impressed, by his courage and bravery to fight what he knew to be a fateful illness. We had enjoyed seven years of a wonderful friendship, and I have many memories and also articles he sent to me in appreciation of the help I had given him and his family. As a result of research and exchange of information, two comrades of Ted Muffitt became known to me. There was Squadron Leader Bruce Daymond, DSO/DFC. RAAF, retired, and Alan Deller ex-RAF, author of the 'Kid Glove Pilot'. The three men had served together on Lough Erne.

The first of the group I made contact with, was Bruce Daymond. In 2002, Bruce was interviewed in Australia by a reporter from BBC Radio Ulster, about his service on Lough Erne. I heard the program, and thought that I should make contact with Bruce, I wrote to Radio Ulster and asked them to forward a letter from me to Bruce, as I knew they could not give me his address without his approval. We corresponded for a number of years until he passed away in May 2008 aged 88 years. I sent him a copy of my Donegal Corridor book, and arranged to get him a copy of 'The Kid Glove Pilot'. During his years of service, Bruce kept a secret diary, from 6th January 1941, when he joined the Royal Australian Air Force (RAAF), until 16th April 1945, when he returned home. He agreed with the diary being typed up and published, in a limited addition for his family and close friends, and provided a copy each to the Australian War Memorial, RAF Museum and Canadian War Museum. Denis Saunders, the son of Eric Saunders, typed up and published the diary. Eric Saunders was Bruce's flying boat captain, when Bruce served with 209 Sqn., RAF, in the UK and Africa, before he took part in his Captains course with 131 OUT at Killadeas. Eric was also with the RAAF, and retired from the air force as a Wing Commander. The Daymond and Saunders families are close friends, and it was Denis Saunders, son of Eric, who typed up the diaries. I was privileged to have been entrusted, on loan, with the diaries, which contained invaluable information on Ted Muffitt.

It was in December 2007, that Norm introduced me to Denis Saunders, and then to Deborah Higginson, who was the daughter of Bruce Daymond. Bruce had passed on his copy of the Donegal Corridor to her brother, Dr. David Cooke. I took it that she would like to have a copy of her own, so I sent one to her. Debbie sent me the following e-mail.

Dear Joe,

Thank you for sending me your book. My brother, Dr. David Cooke, treasures the copy you sent to my Dad. It has been amazing the way the next generation of Muffitt's and Daymond's have become friends as a result of your thorough investigations. As you probably know, David's father, Rolla Cook, was killed in a Spitfire test flight accident, one month before David was born, back in 1941. Rolla and my Dad went to university together, and were great friends. After the war, Bruce Daymond came home, and became David Cook's loving step father. When David and Norm were introduced to each other, they became firm friends. They had much in common - both had lost their fathers, when very young. They shared many flying stories via long 'Skype' conversations, over several years. Norm had been a RCMP pilot in the Canadian outback for thousands of flying hours, and David had been a Flying Doctor in RFDS, in the Australian out back, also for thousands of hours. In a way their careers were very similar – Norm, in freezing icy wastelands and David, in parched deserts. Both felt very close to their fathers in Heaven, especially when flying above the clouds.

Norm keeps in touch regularly, and was so moved when we found a copy of the photo when our Dads did their Captains course, way back in the 1940's. My Dad, Bruce, had asked all participants to sign the back of the photo, and we were thrilled to be able to mail Norm the photo, with his father's original signature, just weeks before my Dad died in May 2008. Dad took great pleasure in communicating with you and Norm before his own death.

My husband Phillip and I, would love to visit you in Ireland one day, and explore the places you have written about. The red kangaroo mascot that my Dad always had in his Catalina cockpit for all his missions, adorns the bookshelf in his old den in his house where we now live. I also am the proud family custodian of Dad's DSO and DFC and other wartime medals of service.

Best wishes from Debbie Higginson (nee Daymond).

****

Bruce was fully experienced in Catalina flying boats. His daring missions earned him both the Distinguished Flying Cross, and the Distinguished Service Order, within a few weeks of each other. The D.S.O. is second only to the Victoria Cross as an air force bravery award. A fourth Burmese mission was the most hazardous. Bruce and his crew were to collect eight allied agents they had earlier delivered behind enemy lines. The agents sent a message that a Japanese submarine had sent out a party ashore to capture them. The orders to Bruce were to rescue the agents "at all costs". Unknown to the agents, the submarine returned at night.

After an eleven hour flight from Madras, Daymond's crew saw the signal that it was safe to alight, and then saw the submarine across their path. Daymond is said to have told his crew, "We can't leave the poor buggers down there", brought the aircraft down near the submarine and taxied at high speed round a headland to pick up the agents. The agents were pulled aboard, the aircraft taxied round the headland, and took off, passing low over the submarine and returned to India safely.

It is remarkable how, after 60 years, and as a result of the 'Search' carried out by Norm Muffitt into his father's accident, that the families of the three men, Ted Muffitt, Bruce Daymond, and Allan Deller, who served together on Lough Erne, should become united in friendship. For me, there were a number of highlights during the ten or so years from Norm first found me. One was the visit to Belleek of Joe Collinson and his wife, Agnes. Another was the welcome visit of Jennifer Jones, Stewart, and Ryan. When the folks returned to Canada, and told Norm and Peg about meeting with me, he told me how much this meant to him. Another highlight was the visit of Debbie Higginson, and her husband, Phillip, to Norm and Peg in Alberta. Even though Norm was aware at this time that there was no hope of recovery from his illness, he and Peg met their Australian friends at the airport, and made them so welcome into their home. Again, Joe and Aggie were there in support of their friends. Such friendships kept Norm in great spirits during a difficult time. He told me how wonderful it was to meet with them. Debbie, who was now in regular contact with me, told me of the great courage of their friend, and how determined he was to fight it out to the bitter end. Debbie suggested to me that I should phone Norm, as we had never spoken to each other. This I did, and had a lovely chat with Peg, before having a wonderful conversation with Norm.

In one of her messages to me, Debbie said, "As Bruce Daymond's daughter, I would like to thank you most sincerely for all you have done to bring peace of mind to the families of so many airmen". I never felt that I was important doing this; rather, I felt that it was a privilege and honour to be an instrument between the spirits of the men who died, and their families. Denis Saunders, son of Eric, has also been in contact with me and contributed valuable information on his Dad and his comrades. It was he who typed up and published Bruce Daymond's wartime diaries and ensured that this important part of history is preserved for future students of the World War 2 years.

CHAPTER 7

Ground crews at Castle Archdale

While it is understandable that flying crews will get more publicity than the men on the ground, most of the flyers will give due credit to those who keep their planes in good condition, for their lives depend on well serviced machines. The following article was penned by A.S.F. Waugh, who served at Castle Archdale.

R.A.F. Station, Lough Erne 1941 – 1942.

Some impressions by 1251737, Waugh, A.S.F. LAC., Station Photographer, from March 20th to June 26th 1941 – 1942.

Foreword.

After the events of Dunkirk, I decided to join the R.A.F. as a photographer. On 24th July 1940, I was accepted into the Volunteer Reserve for the duration of hostilities. On October 25th 1940, I was sent to RAF Palette, near Warrington, for 'kitting out', and from there I was posted to West Kirby in Wirral, on October 31st, for initial training. November 22 saw me in Blackpool, enrolled in No 2 School of Photography. On March 11th 1941, I qualified as an RAF photographer, Second Class. I enjoyed 7 days leave in Bath, (my home town), and was then, on March 20th, posted to RAF, Lough Erne.

The trouble was that no one had ever heard of RAF, Lough Erne. I certainly had not! I had Travel Warrants made out to Irvinestown, in Ulster. Thus I started out on a 48 hour journey to the 'End of the Earth', or so it seemed! By train from Bath, to either Birmingham or Crewe, change, and wait for a train for Carlisle, change again, and wait for a train to Stranraer. Await the Stranraer - Larne ferry, which only sailed at night. Finally, down Loch Ryan, and across to Larne. Train then to York Road Station, Belfast.

On March 19th 1941, I was walking down the Falls Road in "The Dawns Early Light", in full kit and kit bag, it being too early for the trams. Next, to find Great Victoria Street Station, terminus of the Great Northern Railway (Ireland). Now, there are two ways to Irvinestown. The "Quick Way", via Clones in 2 ½ hours to Enniskillen, through the Irish Free State; but if caught, meant 24 hours with the Irish police, and sending back across the border, with a bill for £2, for bed and board (deductible from our monthly salary). This left the "Long way Route", 5 ½ hours. First on the "Derry Train" to Omagh, change for Enniskillen, wait for train. We were now in rural Tyrone, with a horse drawn Tram at Fintona, and another change at Bundoran junction, for the train to Bundoran, in Eire, stopping finally at Irvinestown Station. We would see three clocks showing: - 1, "Railway Time", based on train from Belfast, 2, "Gladstone's Time", being G.M.T., 3, "Gods time", about 2 hours later than London! No. 3 clock made sense, seeing that we were so far west from Greenwich. The latter time was also much favoured by the many public houses.

Duty: Having arrived at our destination, after 2 days travel, with little sleep, we now faced a 2 ½ mile walk up the Kesh Road to Castle Archdale, still in full kit etc. However, the fates were kind that day; an RAF "3 tuner" arrived to pick us up (I was in a party of 4 airmen bound for the unknown). Thus on March 20th 1941, aged 19, I arrived at Castle Archdale headquarters of RAF Station, Lough Erne. Then came another shock; no proper camp, only a few Nissen Huts on a hillside, one of which housed the Squadron Photographers, and to this we were allocated, myself and two Meteorologists. We had no equipment to set ourselves up as tradesmen. We soon learned to keep out of sight to avoid the many "pitfalls" and uncertainties of "General labour". This included filling up wet sacks of wet coal, wheeling the heavy sacks to the Nissen Huts and to Castle Archdale, then unloading them. Stores was one of these general duties. We were soon included on the Guards Register, which meant a wet night out (usually) guarding the depth charges in the Bomb Bays, two hours on four off, armed with a heavy .303 Canadian rifle and bayonet, plus 5 rounds of ammunition. The cartridges were not to be loaded in the rifle. Thus armed we stood or marched up and down under the dripping trees in the dark. On a clear night, there was all of the universe to study - constellations, stars, planets and the Milky Way! I learned them all, and still recall many names memorised on Guard duty.

The first cookhouse was a field kitchen in the open air, where we queued up for our Rations, which many times became diluted with the spring rains, before we could find shelter. We soon learned to look across Lower Erne westwards towards Belleek. If a mist was spotted, we knew we had less than 10 minutes to find some protection from the next storm. With 240 Squadron, and then 209 Squadron Flying Boats, came Squadron photographers, which I joined to help calibrate and check the cameras, removing film etc., for dispatch to RAF Aldergrove. Finally, on April 29th 1941, "Oh Glorious Day", the photo trailer finally arrived. No more General duties apart from fire Piquet's and Guards. Now we could process our own films. The trailer was stationed in the Stables enclosure at the rear of Castle Archdale. The stable buildings housed the Orderly Room and other station offices. Gradually the station expanded, more Nissen Huts, which filled the valley, only to be flooded out in the winter of 1941-1942. We now had a proper dining room; no more wet meals! And a NAAFI recreation room, and a library, where I borrowed my astronomical books for night time study.

Days off meant 7 miles of walking to and from Irvinestown. The older inhabitants called it "Lowtherstown", but I never found out who "Lowther" or "Irvine" was, who gave their name to the locality. The local pleasures were soon enjoyed, however. After the monthly pay parade, when reasonably "flush", we could get an excellent meal of steak, with 2 fried eggs, plus fried potato, and as much bread as we could eat, (5 varieties of bread), with real butter. All hands washed down the meal with tea; all for 1s-6d! Enniskillen proved more expensive, with its cinema and shops, but it meant arranging transport there and back. However, we found everyone very friendly and helpful, ready to accommodate us "Strangers in a foreign land"; albeit we all spoke English. During the spring of 1942, I purchased a wedding ring in Enniskillen, which my wife wears today! We were often paid in Ulster Bank notes. OK in Ulster, but back in Bath, the local banks demurred at changing notes of the Ulster "Linen" Bank etc. I had to wait 5 days for my money; the local shops in Bath refused this unusual currency.

The first Flying Boats were Lerwick's and Sunderland's, followed by the smaller Catalina's of 209 Squadron. Trainee pilots had to prove their ability by finding the tiny piece of rock called "Rockall" out in the Atlantic Ocean, in all kinds of weathers. To prove their capabilities, a photograph was the necessary evidence of sighting; no more difficult than finding a convoy of merchant ships, especially if the convoy had become dispersed. During 1942, we saw units of our American Allies established at Lisnaskea. On occasions, we had to photograph their equipment, etc. This meant lunch in the U.S. air force mess, a lovely meal, but alas, for us, everything was covered in apricot jam, 7lb tins of which were on every table! One day I was called to the Intelligence Office in Castle Archdale, where I and Pilot Officer Mennicker-Meaton had the usual task of sorting out hundreds of photographs, mainly of bridges, in the Free State of Ireland. We had to place them on area maps, record the type of bridge - wooden, stone, brick or steel/iron -, whether railway, road or viaduct, over river, canal, railway, and roads. The idea was to have maps ready in case of a German invasion, plus details of the amount of explosives necessary to deny the bridge to the invader. Fortunately for all concerned, none of this was ever to be used. But we had a lovely week calibrating this material. I often wondered what happened to all these hundreds of postcards, many possibly used.

Living with the "Met" (meteorological) airmen, meant we soon learnt much about weather and forecasting. High pressure meant calm, misty days; low pressure, storms, gales and rain. There would be warm and cold fronts, and best of all, a "Madeira High", which meant lively, warm days, which the locals would call "A heat wave". Alas! We only enjoyed one of these in the 16 months I was there. For some time we were puzzled, when our Flying Boats would disappear westwards, and return from the same direction. Only when I went on a training flight to Rockall, did I learn about the "Donegal Corridor". This was a 10 mile wide part of the Irish Free State, over which we could fly, thus saving a 100 miles extra, round Londonderry and Malin Head in Donegal; very useful when meeting convoys bringing supplies, or outward bound with troops and material for the Middle East and India.

Among all the memories, two stand out in my mind after 60 years. When enough personal arrived at Lough Erne, it was decided to hold weekly Church Parades on Sunday mornings, a "Spit and Polish" occasion, with inspection, parade and march to St. Patrick's Church of Ireland, at the entrance to Castle Archdale. In the RAF, it is a mistake to be enrolled as "C of E", (Church of England). Far better to be enrolled as "O.D.", because "Other denominations" covered many varieties of faith, from Roman Catholic to Jewish tradition. Rarely were enough personnel available for an "OD" parade. However, I was C of E, but this stood me in good stead. St. Patrick's had no electricity, and was not connected to our generators, or the Fermanagh grid. It was lit by oil lamps! Likewise the Church Organ had to be pumped by hand. One of the Squadron photographers could play the piano, and thus the organ, and two of us joined him to pump the organ, raising enough pressure for the music. He was paid 2/6, and we got an extra 6d every time our services were required for practices, and Sunday mornings. Before the Sunday service could begin, we would arrive to prepare and build up the pressure; no parade with "Spit and Polish" for us! Two long wooden handles projected from the organ, which we had to pump up and down. The whole contraption "wheezed and groaned" under our efforts, until sufficient pressure built up, and we could relax to a more gentle application of muscle power.

The Church of Ireland Minister was an "Old Boy", whose favourite sermons included long diatribes against the "Red Communist menace" from Russia, narrowly equalled by warm invective against the "Catholic menace from Dublin". Suddenly, on June 22nd 1941, the "Wicked men of Moscow" became "Our gallant Soviet Allies". Soon after, the Minister disappeared, being replaced by our own RAF Chaplain; no more heated sermons to endure. The second incident included finding a seaworthy rowing boat, which meant with 2 oars "Liberated" from Castle Archdale boat house, we were able to row across and visit various uninhabited islands. At the time, I corresponded with the British Ornithological Society. Thus armed with their forms, we became bird watchers, jotting down all our sightings of Waders, Ducks, Divers, Sea Birds, etc., ranging from humble cots and Dabchicks, to more exotic Great Crested Grebes. One day, for some reason, the Sluice Gates at Belleek were opened, and Lower Erne fell by several feet, exposing one of several reefs. Temptation indeed! Yes, we rowed out to the reef standing several inches above the water level, and standing on the surface, took turns to be photographed, literally standing in the middle of Lough Erne! Unfortunately, we were spotted by those in power. We lost our boat, and any further adventures afloat, but had to do our "Bird Records" from land.

RAF Lower Lough Erne, continued to expand. New units arrived - personnel from Norway and the U.S.A. (after December 1941)-, and besides our Sunderland's and Catalina's, came Boeing Flying Boats. The photo trailer went, because we now had our own static photo section, complete with a Corporal and two Sergeant photographers.

It still took 48 hours to get home on leave, via the short sea crossing Larne to Stranraer. Very often, trains were diverted because of air raids; on one occasion, I finished up in Sheffield, and had to find shelter in the local YMCA, before proceeding to Carlisle, a day late. My wife, Rosina, and I, planned to be married on May 1st, 1942. Arrangements were made, Banns read, reception arranged, and finally, leave obtained. All seemed well in hand. However, during the night of April 25th / 26th, Bath was heavily bombed by the German Air Force, causing over 600 casualties, and extensive damage. I had already left on the 48 hour "Marathon" journey home. En-route, we learned of the raids, so I arrived back in Bath not knowing what to expect, or find! We were lucky, the fates were kind; twice! Rosina had missed being killed by refusing to go into air raid shelters, which were blown to bits. We lost our reception, because of unexploded bombs, but the ceremony, complete on a lovely, sunny, spring day, saw us bound for Torquay on our honeymoon. Today, 60 years later, we are still together. Rosina wears her Irish wedding ring (bought in a jewellers shop in Enniskillen) with pride; despite ups and downs, we have enjoyed a good life.

Epilogue

On June 26th 1942, I was posted overseas, leaving RAF Lough Erne, never to see those misty huts again, or taste "Guinness from the barrel"! On 27th August 1942, the Orient Liner, now a troop transport, "Orcades", a brand new ship, sailed down the Mersey with myself on board having embarked at Bootle. After a glimpse of Malin Head in gathering darkness, I was not to see the British Islands for 3 ½ years. I saw service in Cairo, Egypt, and in Italy, with the Balkan Air Force; but that is another story.

Note:- all dates are correct from my diary, but the details are from memory, now 60 years old.

Signed: - A.S.F. Waugh
January 2002.

****

Another letter sent to the late George Smith in October 2001.

Dear George,

Re: Memories of WW2 LRFHS Oct. 2001. George May.

I was very interested in your references to Castle Archdale on Loch Erne. During WW2, I was a "back room boy" in Radio Dept. RAF Farnborough, and worked on the interference caused by the radars to radio equipment in aircraft. (Also other things).

On the 3rd November 1944, I had to go to St. Angelo's airport, from RAF Northolt, in an Oxford, to look at an interference problem in a PBY(3/), a large aircraft (larger than a Catalina), probably 4 engine. So long ago I can't remember the details. Never got a flight, otherwise I would have the details in my flight log book.

Things like stick in my memory were that there was no blackout, plenty of milk, eggs, bacon. How wet it was (80 inches of rain per annum?) Coming home, standing on a wayside halt, stopping the train by hand signals, changing a warrant at Enniskillen. Problems at Larne, because I was a civilian, so wasn't allowed to travel on the RAF sailing, etc.

Did my first flying in a Catalina, at Beaumaris, Anglesey, Feb. '42, again because of radar interference with Radio receivers. Later on, more flying in Catalina's from RAF Hamworthy. Never got a flight then, in a Sunderland, although I worked on them in WW2. After WW2, when I was involved in the design and flight testing of the L British Directional, Soxo buoy system, I did get a flight in a Sunderland from RAF Calshot, when we had to fly to the RAF Farnborough area, to do measurements on the 60MHz aerial. Later in this development, did quite a lot of work on Firefly, Gaunet, Shackelton.

Yours sincerely,
George May. (M90)

Philip Robblee

In March 2006, I received a request for a copy of my book, from Philip Robblee, who lives in Upsala, Ontario, Canada. I had a very interesting letter, dated 1st April 2006, from Philip, thanking me for the book, telling me how much he enjoyed reading it, and that it contained much that he had never heard about during his service at Castle Archdale. He was there when Sunderland NJ 183 crashed at Knocknagor, and he recalled very clearly that he was on the Guard of Honour for the funerals of the crew, in the Cemetery in Irvinestown.

When he was posted to Castle Archdale, he was at first assigned to light duties; then he was sent to the carpenter's shop, where the F/Sgt. discovered that he was familiar with power tools, as he had worked with his father, who was a carpenter. The sergeant found out that Philip was familiar with the large planner that was there, and a control tower was being built, and windows were needed for it. He made the windows and sashes from wood scrounged by the builders, and they installed the windows themselves. They also cut the glass to keep out the wind and the rain.

He finally cut a finger on a hand saw, and the F/Sgt. terminated his employment in the carpenter shop. He was then sent to work at the trade he had been trained for. He was a member of 8423 servicing echelon, and was assigned to a hanger, and the major overhaul of the aircraft as needed. He was bunked in a Nissan hut, at a gun site on the hill on the road to Kesh. He had been issued with a bicycle, and so was able to travel when not working. He enjoyed his time in Ireland, and met a lot of very nice people. There was an old lady who was crippled, and had a young daughter, who he used take dancing and to the cinema. He lost track of them when he was moved to England, and he was being prepared to go to India, when the war ended. He was then shipped home.

The girls name was Maureen, and he thought that she had relations in Belleek. "If you know of her, say hello from me."

Sincerely yours, Philip Robblee

CHAPTER 8

A New Zealander Returns to Castle Archdale

MY LAST O.B.? By Alfred Frederick (Johnny) Johnston

In mid-January 2006, I was surfing the web looking for information regarding the Irish Free State military camp, called Camp Finner. This was in response to a request from an Anglo Irish lady, whose father and grandfather served there, in the days when the country was controlled by the British. I knew the camp, as during the war, while on secondment from the RNZAF, I was stationed at RAF Station, Castle Archdale on Lough Erne in County Fermanagh, in the north of Ireland. I used to pass it on my way to the seaside town of Bundoran in Donegal. I did not find out much about the Camp Finner, but I came across an item that interested me greatly. It was a 32 page article on a talk on "The Donegal Corridor and Irish Neutrality during World War Two", by Joe O'Loughlin, Local Historian, from Fermanagh, Northern Ireland.

'The Donegal Corridor', so named because it provided a short cut for Catalina's and Sunderland's based on Lough Erne, to fly across that short portion of the Irish Free State territory, from Belleek to Ballyshannon, to access the Atlantic Ocean. Prior to permission being given by the Irish Government, aircraft had first to fly north, and then go around the coast of Donegal, so as to avoid infringement of the neutral Free State Territory. To avoid offending the Germans, and to preserve Irish neutrality, the agreement was secret, and the boundaries of the flight path were clearly defined as to height, and the use of cloud cover. Aircraft were not permitted to fly over Camp Finner. Joe's article aroused my interest, and I learned previously unknown details of the war time activities in the base on which I was stationed. On the last page of the article was an icon of a letterbox with the inscription "If you want to contact Joe, click on the letterbox". I clicked, and sent off an e-mail, explaining who I was, and that I had spent two and a half years, during 1941 to 1943, at Castle Archdale as a wireless operator, and that I had just found his most interesting article on the internet. I had no idea how long the item had been on the internet, or whether or not Joe was still alive.

Much to my surprise, when I checked my e-mail next morning, there was a reply from Joe. He was, as he said, delighted to get mail from New Zealand, and to hear from someone who had served at Castle Archdale during the war years. Over the ensuing months, we communicated on a regular basis. Joe had written a book called "Voices of the Donegal Corridor"; he sent me a copy and wrote "You can pay me when you are here again". That got me thinking, how about it! Could I do it? Go back to my old station after sixty five years? I had a few health problems - very bad feet, difficulty walking far. The more I thought about it, the more I began to think it was on. I checked the possibilities. On the plus side, Joe could arrange accommodation at a bed and breakfast pub in Belleek, at a very reasonable rate. I had a grandson in London, and several friends from way back, in and around the London area, but where would I stay in London? I remembered that during the war, I used to stay at the Union Jack Club at Waterloo, so I e-mailed them. Yes, they still existed and provided accommodation for serving and ex-service people. So after getting a clearance from my doctor, arranging travel plans, insurance etc. it was all go.

It had been a couple of years since I had travelled overseas, and I noticed that the aircraft seemed to be getting larger. How they manage to actually get air borne I am always amazed. The approach to Heathrow was over London, and it was interesting to be able to see various famous landmarks on the way. As expected, there was the usual hassle at Heathrow. I couldn't help but be reminded of my home town airport, Nelson, when I surveyed the baggage carousel snaking its way around the crowded arrival hall, disappearing through a hole in the wall and reappearing a little further away. At Nelson, we have a luggage trolley, which is trundled out with the bags on it; it does a great job! When my turn came at the immigration counter, the tired old lady simply asked me was I visiting relatives or friends. I agreed, and my entry was approved. However, as I exited the "nothing to declare" area, a policeman detached himself from a group who appeared to be keeping an eye on the incoming passengers. He asked me what was the purpose of my visit. I explained that I was visiting my old air force station, and after explaining where that was, I was free to proceed.

I was pleased to see my grandson waiting for me, and as he had been working in London for some time, he knew his way around to a degree, and he guided me through the maze of tube trains, underground walkways, passageways and escalators, to Waterloo station, where we found our way to the Union Jack Club. I spent a few days there, exploring the nearby shops and markets.

During 1963-65, I was attached to the RAF for two years, and was stationed at RAF Signal Command H.Q., at Medmenham, Bucks. I had kept in touch with one of my old neighbours of that time, and after a phone call to say I was back in the country, I was invited down to make a visit to the area. I had been kept informed of the changes at Medmenham, so it was no surprise to see that the lovely old mansion that had been the Officers Mess, was now an upmarket hotel and resort. We were invited to have a look around the establishment, and were very much impressed with it all. RAF Medmenham during the war, housed the Photographic Interpretative Unit, and it was there that they ascertained the location of the launching site of the flying bombs. After a pleasant reunion with my old friends, I returned to London, to do a bit more sightseeing. The principal activity was a tour of London, on an open top bus. A running commentary kept me up with the details of the sights encountered en-route. It is a good way to familiarize oneself with the various famous parts of the city.

The following day, at 06:00, I caught a shuttle bus for Gatwick, to catch the Easy Jet plane for Belfast. After a rigorous security check on arrival, (even the soles of my feet were inspected), I left the arrival hall to find Joe O'Loughlin waiting for me. I had previously suggested that I would find my own way to Belleek, but Joe advised me that if I did it by myself, it would take me all day, and he could do it in a couple of hours. I was pleased to accept his offer of transport. It was a pleasant trip to Belleek, the countryside is certainly green, but it rains a lot! The towns we passed through all looked prosperous, and I could see that there were many improvements since I was there 65 years before. Joe took me to his home on the outskirts of Belleek, where I met his wife and son. After a cup of tea, we were off to my new home for the next fortnight, "The Fiddle Stone", a bed and breakfast pub on the Main Street of Belleek. The next few days were spent with Joe, visiting old wartime aircraft crash sites, and meeting up with his relatives and friends.

Just prior to my departure from N.Z., I had received an e-mail from a researcher, with a television company based in Belfast; they were starting to work on a film for the BBC, about airmen who came to Northern Ireland during the Second World War. The researcher (Jane Veich) visited Joe, and learned that I was coming over, and wanted to meet up with me. Later in the week, Joe and I had a meal in an Hotel in Irvinestown, with the producer, Michael Beattie, of the company, and it was arranged that the team would come over from Belfast to Castle Archdale, the site of the former Flying Boat Base to do some filming.

At the appointed time, Joe and I arrived at Castle Archdale, to find the TV people had arranged to close the Air Force Museum for a period, and had set up their gear there for an interview. The producer was interested in daily life at the base during wartime, and asked me to describe what would be the typical activity I might be engaged in. I told him about how, when our watch would go on duty, we would be briefed by the old watch, would check on the operations board for details of aircraft on patrol, call signs, frequencies, etc., and also its wicker basket of pigeons. This latter item very much surprised my interviewer, just as much as when he learned that we communicated with the aircraft using Morse code. He apologized, saying that he had no knowledge of such things, as all that had happened a long time ago, before he was born. I was beginning to realise how old I was.

After doing a filmed tour of the museum we set off to do some more of the same at the Irvinestown Cemetery, where two RNZAF aircrew are buried. Also buried there, is an RAF wireless operator, LAC H. Ward, one of our signals staff who died in a drowning accident on 17th August 1943. I was present at his inquest and I had attended his funeral as a pall bearer in 1943. We then moved on to Killadeas on Lough Erne, where mainly Catalina's were based. I stood on the jetty gazing out across the water towards the Donegal Corridor and the Atlantic, while they filmed. That seemed to take for ever; I think they had problems with the camera. I decided then, that I would not give up my day job to become an actor. It was however a most interesting day and I very much enjoyed meeting the crew, we got on well together, I especially enjoyed meeting the cameraman, who looked very much like Mick Jagger. I left some old wartime photos and my old RAF identity card, with him. I had forgotten to hand it in when I left the base in late 1943. The T.V. Company will be also visiting the old RAF bases of Ballyhalbert, and Langford Lodge. I have not heard any more of the work on the film, but my friend Joe in Belleek will keep me informed.

Joe looked after me very well during the rest of my time in Ireland. I had discovered just before I left home, that my great grandfather was born in Colooney, County Sligo, not too far away from Belleek, and Joe made sure that we visited that town. We checked out a couple of cemeteries, in the hope that we might find some trace of my forbearers, but found nothing of significance It was, however, quite a feeling to be in the area that my great grandfather once lived. We also visited places like Ballyshannon, Rossnowlagh, Bundoran, Enniskillen and Lough Melvin, and I generally got pretty well acquainted with the area, places I remembered, and some I only formerly had heard the names of. My visit soon came to an end, and Joe took me back to the airport at Belfast, for my trip back to England.

Back in London, I checked in to the Union Jack Club for a few days, but because of shortage of rooms, I had to move on to another services club - The Victory Club, near Marble Arch. I spent a few days there, and then off to Oxford, to visit an old friend, who had recently returned from NZ to be with his family in the UK. I spent an enjoyable time there, meeting up with my hosts family and friends, all of whom made me very welcome, and ensured that I saw the local sights and the countryside. After I returned to London, I visited another old friend, who lives at Richmond. While there, I did the obligatory tour of Kew Gardens, and a nostalgic visit to Trafalgar Square, where I did some 'people watching' for an hour or so; most interesting. Despite notices in various languages, warning people "Do Not Feed the Pigeons", they, the pigeons, were just as numerous as they always were.

The next day, I was off on my return journey to NZ. The first leg of the journey was the most exciting part of the whole return trip. The shuttle bus journey from the Victory Club to Terminal 4 Heathrow, was hair-raising to say the least. I don't know whether or not the driver was running late, but it seemed that there was a determined effort on his part, to get us to our destination in double quick time. At several points on the journey, I was quite amazed that we didn't have a prang! Along narrow streets, with cars parked on both sides, and oncoming traffic, and only one slight bit of road rage evident, when a London cabbie did a U turn right in front of us. Our driver was not amused, and gave the cabbie an earful. I thought we were nearly there, when we arrived at terminal 3, but no, terminal 4 was miles away; but we got there safely in the end. After the usual hassle at the airport, I was on board the aircraft and homeward bound. It was a great trip. I would do it all again, and I have been thinking about the next one.

I had long had an ambition to return to Ireland, where I began my first O.E., and thanks to Joe O'Loughlin, it became possible. Without Joe's help, I could not have made it, and I am most grateful to Joe, his wife Ina, their family and friends, and to the lovely ladies at "The Fiddle Stone", for their warm welcome, and their generous and gracious hospitality.

After returning home, I received an airmail letter from Joe, containing a clipping from the County Fermanagh weekly newspaper, "The Impartial Reporter". It had a half page article headed "New Zealand airman retraces his long journey to Lough Erne". Joe, unknown to me, with his literary talent, had collated information he had gathered from our e-mails, and our talks in Ireland, and together with photographs, had written an article for the paper. I was impressed.

In late 1943, after I had done two and a half years' service in Northern Ireland, I was posted overseas to West Africa, and finished up at RAF Station, Maiduguri, Northern Nigeria. That would be an interesting place to go back to! Coincidentally, a month or so ago, I received an interesting e-mail from a sad young man in Lagos. How he got my address I do not know, but he was in a difficult situation, and pleaded to me for help. It seems that he was heir to a large fortune, and needed to gain access to an overseas bank account, to be able to release his fortune. Apparently, my account would be quite suitable. He would probably be able to help me to get back to my old station in Maiduguri!!!

I WILL THINK ABOUT IT!!!

For me, it was a great experience to have Johnny visit Fermanagh again, and to hear of his life here during the war years. In civilian life in New Zealand, he worked in the Post Office, and became expert in sending telegram messages by Morse code. This was a great foundation for his career in Signals when he joined the RNZAF. He remained in the air force after the war, and served in many countries, until he retired with the rank of Squadron Leader. Jane Veich kindly sent Johnny a DVD of "Tail Wind", and of course he showed it to his many friends in Nelson. Having, before he left NZ, acquired a copy of Breege McCusker's book "Fermanagh and Castle Archdale in World War 2", he was delighted to meet with Breege, and her husband, Seamus. Breege had a chapter in the book on the British boat "The Robert Hastie", which was based at Killybegs, in Donegal. Johnny recalled how he still remembered communicating with the boat, and the code used to descriptor the messages from her crew. Since setting up home at Oakwood Retirement Village, Redmond, near Nelson, South Island, when he retired, he had many friends; one of them, Jocelyn Griffiths, enjoyed making world tours. Jocelyn was due to visit Belleek Pottery with a coach group. Johnny let me know of this, and I met with Jocelyn there, and we had a very pleasant time talking about Johnny.

In June 2011, I had a letter from Johnny, telling me how he had celebrated his 90th birthday, on 9th June. Some years before hand, he had made an agreement with his niece, Mary Johnston, whose birthday was a day before his, that together they would make a parachute jump. In a Skydive Abel Tasman plane, they flew to 16,000 feet and from that height made the jump. All his friends and relations were present to witness the event. The local newspaper "The Nelson Mail", heard about it and published the story with photographs.

Another friend of Johnny's was Mrs. Isobel Doddington, known as Dee. Her grandfather and father had served in Finner Camp, (the place mentioned above by Johnny), when it was a British Military Camp. When my friend, retired Colonel Declan O'Carroll, wrote a history of Finner Camp, I sent a copy of it to Dee. Declan had been O.I.C. in Finner for some years, and his father had also served there after it was handed over to the Irish Government about 1924.

Dee wrote and told me how interesting it was for her to see a photo in the book of her Barton grandfather, which she had never seen before. Dee herself joined the British army during World War 2. While stationed in Palestine in 1942, she met with a Pat Mac Rory, who was mentioned in the Finner book. She and Pat would tell people how their fathers had served in the 10th Inniskilling's during the First World War. Dee told another interesting story about a "Sam Browne" belt. Her father had acquired a Sam Browne belt when in the Donegal Militia, and wore it in the 1914-19 war. In the 1920 Troubles in Ireland, an IRA man. B......S........, arrived at their family's kitchen, and asked for her father. He said he was a Major General in the local Rebel group, (quite a high rank real or imaginary), and wanted to borrow Barton's Sam Browne belt. He was having an important parade of his men, and the Sam Browne belt would make him look more official. The belt was handed over. Dee Doddington joined the British Forces in WW2, and was serving in Egypt in the Red Cross. Her father asked B...... S.......... for the Sam Browne belt back, got it, and forwarded it to his daughter in Egypt. Dee brought the belt to NZ, and after hearing the story, an ex-army resident of the village here, suggested that she donate it to the NZ Army Museum, and there it now resides.

While still in the army, Dee arrived back in Northern Ireland on leave. There was difficulty in crossing the border in uniform, from Derry to go to Portsalon, Co. Donegal, Eire, where the family lived. The bus driver solved her problem, by advising her to take off her tunic, and fold it over, concealing the military insignia. She and the driver got talking on the journey, and she told him that she was on her way from Italy. He asked her had she been to Rome, and she said how she had been with a group chosen to have an audience with the Pope. The Pope came to her, and spoke with her; she told him that she was Church of England, and the Pope told her that was no problem, and gave her his blessing. The driver told the story in Portsalon, and Dee became quite a celebrity locally, having had an audience with the Pope.

I had an e-mail from Johnny, to tell me that Dee Doddington had passed away on 12th December 2010. Another story also came to light; one of Dee's Grandfathers was a Dr. Johnston, who owned one of the few motor cars in Donegal, in the early 1920's. A local group of Rebels had a plan hatched that required a motor car. A local man William Gillespie wrote a song to record the event.

JOHNSTON'S MOTOR CAR

Down by Brockagh Corner one morning I did stray,
When I met another rebel bold, who this to me did say;
I've orders from the Captain to assemble at Dunbar,
But how are we to reach Dungloe without a Motor Car?

O! Barney dear be of good cheer and I'll tell you what we'll do.
The Black and Tans have plenty guns altho' we have but few.
We'll wire down to Stranorlar before we walk so far,
And we'll give the boys a jolly ride on Johnston's Motor Car.

When Johnston got the wire, then he soon pulled on his shoes,
He says the case is urgent, there's little time to lose.
He wore a fancy castor hat and on his breast a star.

You could hear the din going through Glenfin of Johnston's Motor Car.
When he came to the Reelin Bridge, he met some rebels there.
He knew the game was up with him, and at them he did stare.
He said "I've got a permit for travelling out so far".
You can keep your English permit, but we want your Motor Car.
What will my loyal comrades say, when I get to Drumboe?
To say my car was commandeered by Rebels from Dongloe.
We'll give you a receipt for her; it's signed by Captain Maher,
And when Ireland's free, then we will see to Johnston's Motor Car.

They put the car into motion; they filled it to the brim,
With guns and bayonets shining, while Johnston he did grin.
When Barney waved a rebel flag, she shot off like a star,
And they gave three cheers for freedom and for Johnston's Motor Car.

When the loyal crew, they heard the news, it grieved their hearts full sore.
They swore they'd have reprisals before they would give o'er.
In vain they searched through Glenties, the Rosses and Kilcar,
While the Rebels their Flags displayed on Johnston's Motor Car.

Two of Johnny's New Zealand comrades are buried in the Irvinestown War Graves:

Sergeant Francis Augustine Weaver, was born in Dunedin on 1st November 1914. He enlisted on 13th April 1941, and after early training, he was sent to Canada, and there was awarded the Wireless Operator Air Gunner Badge, and promoted to Sergeant. He was sent to Nova Scotia to complete his training, and allocated to the Royal Air Force Transport Command, operating between Canada and the United Kingdom.

Sergeant Weaver was a member of the crew of a Ventura aircraft, engaged on the 28th August 1942 in a flight from Derval to the U.K. The aircraft was last heard of when an S.O.S. message was received at 08:21 G.M.T., stating that it was flying on only one engine. It is presumed to have gone down in the sea. When it failed to arrive at its destination, all the crew including, Sergeant Weaver, aged 27, were classified as missing. Later his body was washed ashore at Clooney, Co. Donegal, Eire. He is buried in the Sacred Heart Catholic cemetery, in Irvinestown, Co. Fermanagh.

Warrant Officer Edward Lindsay Darrell, RNZAF W/O, aged 22, died on 21st September 1944, as a result of a drowning accident, when he fell over board from a rowing boat, on Lough Erne, near Boa Island. His body was recovered at 17:00 on the following day, about 10-15 yards from the shore, in the town land of Mullins, Boa Island. He is buried in the Church of Ireland Cemetery, Irvinestown.

The town of Irvinestown is to the north of County Fermanagh, about 12 miles from Enniskillen. The Church of Ireland, where 75 young air men are buried, is on the road to Lisnarick. A short distance along the road is The Sacred Heart Catholic Church, where 11 more young men are buried. A special section of the C.O.I. cemetery, to the left of the entrance, was set aside for service war graves. As time went on, additional burial ground became necessary, and a section against the south wall, about 25 metres from the first, was also set aside. They are linked by a path, and form a war graves section with its own entrance gate. A Cross of Sacrifice has been erected to the right of this gate, immediately in front of the first group of graves, and along the path facing the other group, is a seat. All the graves are in level, closely mown grass, and are marked by headstones of the traditional Commission design.

PHOTO GALLERY

Fl/Lt. Douglas Dolphin and his wife June.

Caricature by Jennifer Muffitt/Jones, of the Author, Joe O' Loughlin.

Ceremony for Dolphin crew at Mahoo Jetty.

Handley Page Hampden Bomber.

- 85 -

Crew of Sunderland DP181.

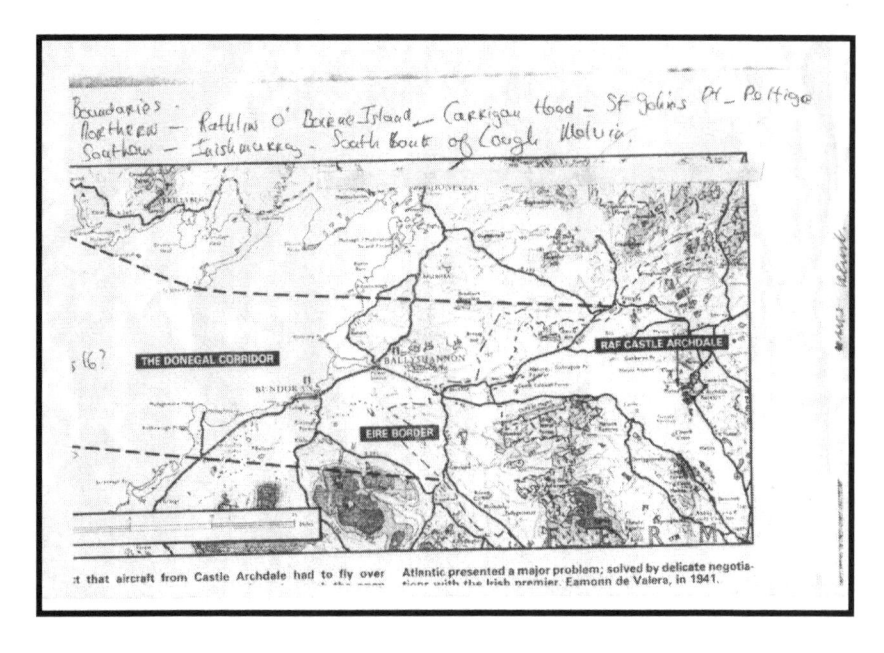

Map of Donegal Corridor.

*The late Lieutenant General Dermot Early, Chief of Staff,
Irish Defence forces, with the author.*

A Catalina Flying Boat.

A Sunderland Flying Boat.

17 August New Zealand High Commissioner Sir William Jordan visited Castle Archdale, with Sir William is the station commander Group Captain Pearce and members of the RNZAF based in the area, The Waaf officer was a New Zealander serving in the RAF and based there. 2nd from right Johnny Johnston.

Ken Lunn, Ex. RAF Castle Archdale.

Les & Maureen Ingram at headstone of Fl/Sgt. Joseph W. Burton, member of crew of Sunderland DD848.

Sharon Trogdon and daughter Claudia at Bundoran Halifax memorial.

Mayor Jim Quinn, Millville, New Jersey and his wife Kimberly at the Grann memorial.

The Memorial plaque for the crew of the B17 flying fortress that crashed on the 'Folly Field' near the Grann Monastery.

The late Doreen Bastick, a member of WAAF, who served in signals at Castle Archdale.

The wreckage of the Boeing B17 no 231468 that crashed at the Grann (2 of).

Another picture of the B17 wreckage,

The Abbeylands, Ballyshannon Historical Group for Liberator B24.

The crew of Catalina JX242 that crashed at Lough an Laban, near Lough Erne.

Fl/Lt. Tom Allitt Captain of Sunderland that crashed on Mt. Brandon.

Lac Phillip Roblee, RCAF. Ground Staff at Castle Archdale.

Katie Frazer, daughter of Capt. Tom Allitt makes her first visit to her father's grave after learning the true facts of his crash in Kerry.

The BOAC civilian version of the Sunderland as flown by Tom Allitt.

Bob Singer, Chuck Singer, the late Frank Garvin, ex RAF and Dr Edward Daly. Retired Bishop of Derry and native of Belleek.

The Catalina AH536 memorial stone at Castle Archdale.

A U.S. Army jeep as used in World War II.

The memorial service at Ely Lodge for the crew of Catalina JX252. From left: James McLaughlin, Pat Donnelly, RAFA, Jack Gilmour, his wife and daughter, relations of crew member at memorial stone.

The Memorial Stone at the crash site of Catalina JX 252.

The Memorial to the crew of Catalina AM265 that crashed on Anaugh Hill, Glenade, Co Leitrim on 21st March 1941.

The Memorial Stone to the crew of Catalina AH551 is unveiled at Whitehall, Ballinamallard by Fl/Lt. Peter Moffatt, 422 Squadron Ass. RCAF, and LAC Wes. Maxwell, 422 Sq. Ass. RCAF. In the background are Sgt. Pat Donnelly, Omagh Branch of RAFA and F/O Terry Reeves, 422 Sq. Ass. RCAF.

- 99 -

F/O Guy Wilkinson who died in the crash of Sunderland DD848 on Mt. Brandon, Co Kerry on 4th August 1943.

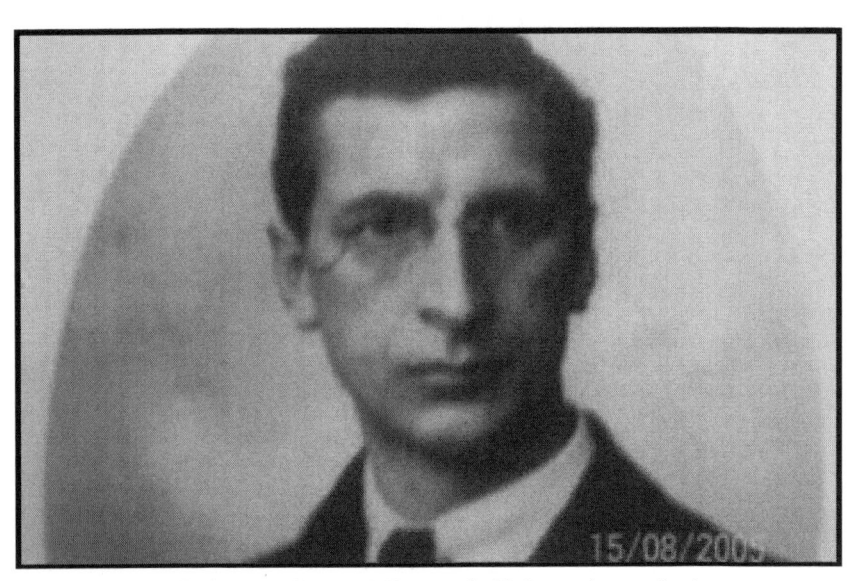

Irish Taoiseach (Prime Minister) Eamon de Valera who made the agreement with Sir John Maffey for the use of the Donegal Corridor.

Jennifer Muffitt/Jones, Commodore Mary Anne Sutton, Lough Erne Yacht Club with the author at a wreath laying ceremony at the club.

St. John's Point Look Out Post, Co Donegal taken from a Sunderland. See look out post number and large EIRE.

Left to right: Mayo Murphy, Camera crew man, Paul Clark, UTV, Breege McCusker, Colonel Michel Legault, RCAF, Joe O'Loughlin, Loouise Williams and the late Noel Ingram.

Memorial to crew of Catalina FP239 that crashed at Reaghan Hill, Omagh, Co Tyrone on 30th Dec 1942.

CHAPTER 9

Ex-RAF Officers Visit Lough Erne

The story of ex RAF officer, **Sgt. George Smith**, is told in a chapter in my Donegal book. An account of the visit of **Sgt. Ken Lunn**, is told later in this chapter.

Sadly, **George Smith** passed away on 9th June 2009, aged 89 years. At his funeral on Jersey Island, one of his friends spoke in tribute to George. Here are a few fitting extracts from that tribute:

We have gathered here today to pay our own tribute to our friend George, and I am sure we will all remember different things about his personality and ways, that he will leave in our minds. He was very proud, and rightly so, of his service career, which was the best part of his long life. Especially the years he spent in Gibraltar and Ireland, working on Catalina Flying Boats. His great hobby was researching the history of what happened many of the aircraft that were stationed in these areas. Prior to George's work, there was little record of details of the tragedies that had taken place, and so many families were left with the usual inadequate telegram, "Missing, presumed dead".

Thanks to George's work, many of the families now have so much more knowledge as to the real fate of their loved ones. In the Donegal Corridor book, many tributes are paid to him for all that he has achieved in this respect. Even after all this time, people's minds are put at ease by being able to put a closure to their grief. Two of the high lights of the later years of George's life, were return visits to Gibraltar and Castle Archdale, in Ireland. With the help of the Royal British Legion, and the Royal Air Force Association, he had also been able, every year, to attend the Remembrance

Service at the Cenotaph in London, ably assisted by his friend, Roberto, and his wife. This has made the last years of his life fulfilled; to be able to present his Poppy wreath in the parade was such an honour for him, and for all his friends. Finally, thanks were expressed to Matron Liz Booth, and the staff of Maison le Cordie, the home where George was so well cared for, at the end of his life.

George referred many of the people seeking information to me; as I live in the area, he knew that I could get, and provide, much information. Maybe in his own, way he was grooming me to replace him, and carry on the good work he started. In recent years, a number of students preparing for their history examinations have contacted me for the history of WW2 in this part of Ireland. They now have a duty to pass on the history to future generations, and carry on the work started by George Smith. One e-mail he sent to me, was a copy of one from a Mark Irvine, who lives in Co. Down, N. Ireland. He said, "Having found your website and read of your experiences, it was all of special interest to me. I grew up in Ballyshannon, where my father was the Presbyterian Minister. On many occasions he was called out to administer spiritual aid to the young air men who died in the plane crashes".

Another interesting letter to George was from a Stanley Smith, who lives in Canada. He wrote: "I had a couple of experiences at Castle Archdale, which are memorable to me. The first, was one morning when I was walking from the living quarters to the base with a group of airmen. We were walking up this hill, with the road to the headquarters just above, when a WAAF Officer suddenly appeared, riding her bicycle. She fell off the bicycle, and the airmen with me managed to catch her, but not before we had a gorgeous split-second view of green knickers. Far from being grateful for being rescued from her fall, she was furious, probably at being touched by such lower life forms.

The second experience I had, was when I was sent on crash guard duties to a mountain, about 10 miles west of Archdale, and on the south shore of Lough Erne. The squad reached the crash site in the evening, and it turned out to be a Catalina JX242, which had hit the top of the mountain near a small lake, Lough an Laban, while circling to land in the early hours of the morning. There were two survivors of the crash, and they had apparently jumped out of the blisters when it hit. If the aircraft had been flying just 20 feet higher, it would have cleared the mountain. The next morning, the rescue squad left to carry the bodies down the mountain, while I was detailed with another airman to stand guard over the crash site. We were given Sten guns, but no ammunition, and we were told we could leave after 2 days. This was the first time I had ever been on top of a mountain in Ireland, and was amazed to find that the ground was just as swampy as where we were, at lower levels. At night, the methane gas coming out of the ground was spitting and sparking. While we were there, an armament officer came, and detonated the depth charges lying there from the crash. When we left the mountain, and were going down to the highway, we came to a deep creek, and the airman with me threw his Sten gun, which instead of landing on the other side, landed in the creek. We decided to leave it there, and in due course, reported that he had lost it. A month later, I was called in, and asked if I could remember where the Sten gun might be, in the creek. I indicated that I knew the place, and accompanied the police out to the spot. I pointed to the creek, and the policeman reached down into the creek, and lifted out the Sten gun. I think the police were concerned that the Sten gun might fall into the hands of the IRA. While at Archdale, I married a girl from Enniskillen, and when the war was over we moved to Canada in 1948.

Sgt. Ken Lunn: Ken was a WOP/AG. He served on 1402 Flt,. at Aldergrove, N. Ireland, in 1943, on Hampden's and Hudson's, and in 518 Sqn., on Halifax's, in 1943/44. As a result of my involvement with the memorial stone and remembrance service to the crew of Halifax LK 704, of 518 Squadron, which crashed at Bundoran on 23rd January 1944, I became acquainted with Ken Lunn. Having flown in Halifax's with the same squadron, Ken knew several of the crew who died in this crash. I sent Ken the details of the ceremony, and he said in a letter to me "The photographs of the area, together with the newspaper reports of the event, has given me a very good picture of what has been happening. I would like to think that I could pay a visit to see the memorial site, perhaps next spring". So plans were put in place for the visit of Ken back to Ireland, after over sixty years.

Following his visit, he contributed an article to "CONSTANT ENDEAVOUR", the Newsletter of the Coastal Command and Maritime Air Association journal, Number 13, Spring 2004. A former member of 518 Squadron, Peter Rackliff, who, with his wife Pam, had attended the ceremony at Bundoran, had contributed an article to an earlier edition of the journal. Peter was a member of the Meteorological Squadron, and Halifax LK 704 was on a Met mission when it crashed.

CONSTANT ENDEAVOUR

"Inspired by Peter Rackliff's article, in Issue 11 of the Newsletter, concerning the Bundoran Memorial to the 518 Sqn. Halifax crew, I decided it was time I went back to Northern Ireland, as it was sixty years since my last visit. I duly took a flight from Gatwick to Belfast City Air Port, where I was met by Joe O'Loughlin. (More of Joe's work later). He had kindly driven all the way from Belleek in Fermanagh, (240 mile round trip), to pick me up, and act as my guide for the next four days.

There was little point in spending time at 5 OUT Magheraberry, as that establishment had long since been turned into a prison. Aldergrove, too, where I spent most of 1943, is now an international airport, and bears no resemblance to the old RAF base of WW2. So we travelled west towards Enniskillen, and I was surprised to see the old RAF base at St. Angelo was still there, used as a local holiday airport, but closed early in 2003. As my log book shows, it was a very handy place to put down with a U/S engine.

I was well looked after at the hotel in Belleek, and during the next few days covered, many miles looking at sites of interest. I never knew if I was in N.I. or the Republic, as the border twists and turns so much. I was pleased to have taken both Sterling and Euros, as small towns on the border could not make up their minds which currency they should deal with. Most house wives carried two purses.

A visit to the memorial to the crew of Halifax LK 704, revived many memories. I contributed some of the background information to the historians involved in the project. Our crew had completed an 11 hour trip in this aircraft, just 24 hours before its last flight. I do remember that the weather conditions in January 1944 were terrible. We were informed on one trip, that we were the only aircraft airborne in the U.K. (not what we wanted to hear at the time). So I can appreciate the many problems this unfortunate crew experienced.

Flying boat members might be interested to know that a number of memorial stones have been erected in the wonderful countryside overlooking Lough Erne. When this is done, families have been notified, and invited, where possible, to attend a memorial service. Castle Archdale is now a holiday caravan and boating site, but the old slipways and large retaining rings sunk into the concrete are still there. It also has a museum to the local countryside pursuits, but about half is given over to an R.A.F. Museum, where I was able to purchase a book called "Castle Archdale and Fermanagh in

WW2", by historian Breege McCusker, printed by Necarne Press, Drumharvey Irvinestown, Co. Fermanagh, BT94 1ET. There are many old photographs and illustrations, a must for the waterborne air force!

There are some unveiling ceremonies due, which will have taken place by the time you read this. Details of the plaques are below. Necarne Castle is now an equestrian park, but some might remember it was a 500 bed RAF hospital, used by both the RAF and American forces. I was much impressed by the good work being done, by Joe O'Loughlin, Breege McCusker, and their helpers, who came from both sides of the border. Not only do they act as guide and mentor to the likes of me, they spend much time corresponding with people all over the world who wish to have further information regarding the fate of a family member many years ago. The hard work engraving, and placing these memorial stones, on, or adjacent to, crash sites, is no easy task, and we owe these good people our grateful thanks. Members of the family of W/O Ernest Slack, who died when Catalina JX 242 crashed on the 20th November 1944, on a mountain top overlooking Lough Erne, were present for the unveiling ceremony of the stone in memory of that crew. The local Churchill and Tully Castle Historical Society, in co-operation with Breege McCusker, Irvinestown, and Joe O'Loughlin Belleek, have, with the permission of the Forest Service, placed a memorial stone with the names of the dead airmen inscribed on it, at the Lough Navar Viewpoint. There is also a metal post at the actual crash site, with a similar inscribed plaque on it.

Ken Lunn

****

On Thursday, November 18th 1943, Sunderland W4036 of 201 Squadron, R.A.F. Castle Archdale, crashed into Lough Erne, off the Point of Mahoo. Three of the crew died in this crash. Two of the bodies are believed to be still on board this plane, and it is a recognised War Grave, lying in over 200 feet of water. The aircraft was engaged on local flying, and crashed during a landing exercise; details of this crash are in an earlier chapter. A stone that matches the one for JX242, has also been placed at the View Point. It commemorates the crew of W4036, and all other airmen who died while serving on Lough Erne, during World War 2. The Fermanagh Flying Boat Association, and The Church Hill and Tully castle Historical Society, joined with members of the Slack family, at a memorial service and unveiling of the stones, on 17th August, at 2-30pm. The Church Hill Sliver Band was in attendance; over 300 people attended the service. By the time this edition is published, a third engraved stone will be in a position, commemorating Catalina AH536, of 240 Squadron RAF Killadeas, which crashed off Gay Island, Castle Archdale, on Wednesday 7th May 1941, at 04:30 hrs. Ten crew members died, and nine bodies are still aboard; it is the second War Grave in Lough Erne. This stone was unveiled in a moving ceremony, in May 2006. Mrs. Pauline Martin, Edinburgh, a cousin of the Pilot, Fl. Lt. Peter Thomas, was present at the ceremony.

This was another memorable trip back to Fermanagh for an airman. Back home, on several occasions, Ken has given talks to members of the Air Crew Association. They were both surprised, and amazed, to learn the facts about the involvement of the Irish people in World War 2, and how local groups ensured that the men who lost their lives here, will be remembered for all time, and commemorated by memorial stones. Most of the A.C.A. members had served in Bomber Command, and had no idea of the work done by Ken, and his comrades, in the Battle of the Atlantic, which was the longest battle of WW2. Ken said that at least now they know where the Donegal Corridor is, and about the great work being done in Ireland. He at one time sent me a lovely tea towel, which is not used for the purpose for which it was originally intended. It has illustrations of most types of planes that served on Coastal Command, and when I give lectures on the period, I use it, along with models of the aircraft and other artefacts, to show the audiences.

Ken Lunn was pretty well known in ex-servicemen's circles. In March 2008, I had a letter from a Bill Kerr, seeking information of a plane that crashed in Glendowan, Co. Donegal. Bill is a retired Customs Officer, and one of his colleagues, Bob McGill, was an ex- RAF service man. Bill was born in Glasgow, and during the war, he was evacuated, as a four year old, to live with his grandmother in Glendowan, Co. Donegal. During his time there, an RAF aeroplane crashed on Glendowan Mountain. He asked Bob how he should go about getting information on the crash. Bob recommended that he contact another friend, ex-RAF man, Ken Lunn, who lived in Surbiton. Ken, in turn referred, Bill to me as a good source of information on crashes in Donegal, where at least 40 Allied planes had crashed during the war. About 200 planes had crashed in neutral Ireland, from 1939 to 1945. Bill wanted to find out if the crew survived, and if so, were they interned, or did they get across the border, with the help, or despite, the hostility of the locals. (There

CHAPTER 10

Relatives of Crew Members

As a result of the website being set up, and information found by research in Fermanagh and other parts of Ireland, the following contacts were made by families who lost loved ones in crashes, or other incidents, involving air craft in Ireland. Prior to this, all the families had was an inadequate telegram telling them that a loved one was either missing, or killed in action. To get the real facts was a great comfort to the relations, and also brought a sense of closure to an important chapter in family history.

Information from the files of Dennis Burke, James Stewart, Tony Kearns, George Smith and Breege McCusker was most valuable in compiling this list.

Officer	Plane	Crash site	Relationship
Fl/Lt Peter C. Thomas	Catalina AH536	Gay Island, L. Erne	Mrs. Pauline Martin, cousin Danny Hodgetts, cousin.
W/O Edward Knibbs	Sunderland NJ183	Knocknagor	Eve Ward, cousin.
F/O James R. Seeger	Sunderland NJ183	Knocknagor	
W/O Jean Marie Soucie	Sunderland NJ183	Knocknagor	Don Soucie, nephew.
F/O Terence Hailstone	Sunderland NJ183	Knocknagor	

Some of the remaining members of 423 squadron, led by Lieutenant Colonel Bruce Ploughman, and relations, visited the site in recent years.

Officer	Plane	Crash site	Relationship
F/Lt. Ted Muffitt	Catalina FP120	Rockall Island	Norm Muffitt, son Jen Muffitt, granddaughter Hester, his wife Monda, his daughter.
P/O Glyn Norman Gzowski	Halifax LK 704	Bundoran	Jane Moore Glynn Warrick, nephew, Kingston, Canada.

Glyn's body fell into the sea, and was never recoverd.

Officer	Plane	Crash site	Relationship
F/O Clarence Scott RCAF	Halifax LK 704	Bundoran	Dianne Jackson, niece, Alberta, Canada

Officer   Plane   Crash site   Relationship

Officer	Plane	Crash site	Relationship
Sgt.F.C.E. Hussey	Halifax LK 704	Bundoran	Eric and Peter Robinson, nephews.

Brian Booth, Wiltshire, retired weather forecaster, made contact re- Halifax LK 704

Officer	Plane	Crash site	Relationship
Sgt. Harold R. Jeal	Sunderland NJ175	Cashelard/Belleek	Leon Jeal, son, his brother and sister.
Sgt. Charles Singer	Sunderland NJ175	Cashelard/Belleek	Bob Singer son and daughters.
W/O John S. Kelly	Sunderland DD859	Shot down by U-Boat U-489	Morna Irwin, niece.
F/O D.M. Wettlaufer via	Sunderland DD 859		Barbara Greyson George Smith.
F/Sgt Alfred F. Sherry RAAF.	Catalina FP193	Boa Island L. Erne 9th Jan.1944	Margaret and Rod Gallagher, niece.

Two Crew missing from this crash were Sgt. Harry Bagley and Sgt. Ed. Leroy Gros

Officer	Plane	Crash site	Relationship
P/O Rodney W. Smith	Sunderland W3977	Donegal Bay	Danielle Hurley grand-niece.
Sgt. Ronald H. Oldfield	Catalina AM265	Glenade	Gladys and Maurice Duffill, nephew.
Sgt. Henry Dunbar	Catalina AM265	Glenade, Co. Leitrim	Harry Dodd, nephew.

Officer	Plane	Crash site	Relationship
Captain Tom Allitt	Sunderland G-ages	Mt. Brandon,	Kerry, Katie Frazers, daughter.
Sgt. Lawrence Quinn	Sunderland ML823	Bloody Foreland	Patsy Quinn, Norman, cousin.

Officer	Plane	Crash site	Relationship
F/O Delmar Ronald McGilliveray	Halifax MZ 980 Feb.9th '45	Mullaghmore Bay, Co. Sligo	Dara and Gail Robertson, niece.
Sgt. Edwin Watson	Sunderland ML760	Bay of Biscay	Mark Allan, Grandson.
Sgt. Elvet Parry	Sunderland W4036	Lough Erne	Mrs. Mary Garston & Ida Mould, North Wales, sisters.
Sgt. John Bosanko Green	Sunderland W 4036		Mrs. Aine Hind, England, sister.
F/Lt. Douglas Dolphin	Sunderland W4036	Lough Erne	Bob Dolphin, Brother and family.
W/O Norman Gardner	Halifax EB134	Tuam, Galway	Wing Com. David Frederick, cousin.

Bruce Johnston, brother of Flight Sargent A.S. Johnston, (Tuam Halifax), visited Belleek and Irvinestown.

Officer	Plane	Crash site	Relationship
Fl.Sgt. George E. Jones	Catalina W8418	Pembroke Dock, Wales	Vivian Williams, cousin.
Sgt. Leslie Rowe	Catalina Z2148	Shetlands, Scotland	Dr. John Rowe, cousin.

Rev. R.A. Knox, Sullen Voe, sent details of the crash

Officer	Plane	Crash site	Relationship
Sgt. James McAvoy	Sunderland ML743	Killybegs, Donegal	Helen McGloin Grand-niece.
Sgt. Phillip R. Field	Sunderland W4000	At sea beside Shipping convoy	Arthur Field, cousin.
P/O Arthur Webster	Sunderland W4000	At sea beside Shipping convoy	Ian Meadows, cousin.

Officer	Plane	Crash site	Relationship
Sgt. H.H. Newbury	Catalina AM265	Glenade, Leitrim	Selwyn Johnston, friend.
Sgt. Arthur Whitwam	Catalina FP114	Missing at sea, Gibraltar 4th August 1943	David Smith, nephew.

Fl/Lt. Hugh Kenneth Mackey aged 31 died suddenly at Killadeas on 12th July 1942.

Lt. Marvin James Reddick survived a Liberator crash, in Ballyshannon, County Donegal. His son, James Reddick

P/O John Bartlett	Sunderland W3977	Donegal Bay	Anny Pritchard, niece & Molly Pritchard, sister.

F/O Frederick W. Greenwood's plane, Sunderland ML823, crashed off Bloody Foreland, County Donegal. His body was found on the shore near Killybegs, by Margaret Gallagher's father. W/O R.H. Voyce survived crash.

W/O Ernest Slack	Catalina JX242	Lough an Laban	Kathryn Slack, Peter and Tony, Albert Slack and family.
P/O. Maurice V Waring	Sunderland DW110	Blue Stack Mountains County Donegal	Dyan Tucker, cousin, New Zealand.
F/O Harold Seward 21	Catalina AM365	Glenade	Ken Rimell Boshan, Cousin.
Fl/Lt Fl/Lt. Francis Wilfred Smith	Sunderland W3977	Donegal Bay	Jon Barker, cousin.
W/O David T Williams	Pilot in Catalina's at C.A.	No injuries	Brian T. Williams, Son.

Sunderland ML883, was sunk at Calshot when hit by boat, but there were no casualties. Enq. John Greenwood.

A/C1 David Pullar was drowned in Lough Erne when Pinnace boat sank. Stephan Pullar, nephew.

Sgt. Robert Dickie, 201Squadron, was injured in accident. Died in County Hospital on 4th April 1945. Robert Dickie, son.

Lac. John Sherwood served at Castle Archdale. No incident. Grandson, Jason Sherwood.

Sgt. Douglas W. Nater. Catalina JX 242. Lough an Laban. An enquiry from home town, Ilford, Essex, was submitted by Andy Spiller. (Roll of Honour)

P/O Arthur E. Field. Sunderland ML 823 crashed off the Donegal coast. An enquiry was made by Jean M. Field, his wife.

P/O Arnold Card died March 15th 1943. No Details available. Enquiry made by Laurie Russell, Canada.

LAC Henry A. Cottam, 18. Catalina AH536 crashed on Gay Island, Lough Erne. Enquiry made by Rev. Andy Herrick, cousin.

Catalina AH532 failed to return from Atlantic patrol on the 21st April 1941. Crew members Sgt. Horace Arthur Tann, aged 20, and F/Sgt. Alfred Tizzaerd, aged 26, were killed in the crash. The body of Fl. Sgt. Tizzard was found of the coast of Galway, and is buried in Kilmurvey (Knockaman) graveyard, on Innismore, one of the Aran Islands of the coast of County Galway. F/Sgt. Tann is buried on Cruit Island Catholic Cemetery, Co Donegal. Enquiry from Martyn and Bernadette Attwell.
Crew missing: - F/Lt. Henry F. Dempster Breese, aged 23; W/O Clifford Bond, aged 28; F/Sgt. Leslie Stewart Dilnutt, D.F.M., aged 31; Sgt. Walter Henry Balce, aged 19, Sgt. Alexander Vaughan McRae; AC2 Herbert Vernon Norton, aged 20; and AC1 James Frank Woodward.

F/O Erik William Breadkstad, RAF, (Admin and Special Duties Branch), kept a photo album with pictures of places where he had served. The album was bought by Oliver Clutton-Brock who contacted me, and James Stewart, to get our help in identifying the photos of Castle Archdale and Lough Erne. This we were pleased to do.

A garden seat in memory of the late Bill Parker, RCAF, is placed on the shore at Castle Archdale.

F/O Faine M. Doyle went down with the Liberator, which was lost at Meeks,

Iceland, on the 16th Sept.1943. The Base was Nutts Corner. Lisa Millar, his grand-niece. (15th June 2011)

F/O Hugh Magee died in a crash in the Mourne Mountains. He is buried in Carrickfergus. David and Jane Hill, from New Zeeland, a nephew.

F/O Arnold Sidney Cruttenden, died in Liberator crash near Innistrahill, Donegal coast on 13th July 1944. Enquiry from Ian Cruttenden.

F/O. Arnold Card, died in Liberator crash near Eglington Base, on the 15th March 1943. He is buried at St. Canice Church of Ireland, Faughanvale, Eglington, Derry. Enquiry from Laurrie Russel.

Orville Lewis, U.S.A. tells of two brothers who were Church ministers. F/O William Milton and F/O Marshall Milton, were both pilots in the U.S. air force in Europe.

The Catalina AH545 that had spotted the Bismarck failed to return from a mission in the Atlantic on 15th July 1942.

Susan Garrett, Kilkenny made enquiry about a B17 Flying Fortress that crash landed near Johnstown, without a crew on board. The crew had bailed out at Ballinamallard, Fermanagh and the plane flew south on auto-pilot before crashing.

Enquiries from Judy and Cressida Ruby, relations of Carlos Maestas, a survivor of Abbeylands Liberator.

Also from Marvin Reddick, son of Arnold Reddick, and relation of Dan Grieber. Also from Tyler Raby, whose uncle was in the Liberator.

Enquiry from Keith Talby, about a Catalina crash in Ireland. A Mr Dunn survived the crash. A Sgt. Dunn is mentioned in John Pickin's website. No details of a crash.

Sgt. Donal Mudd, aged 28, Catalina AH551, Whitehill, 16th Oct. 1943. James Stewart had an enquiry from nephew.

Flight Lieutenant F.G. Fellows, a crew member of Sunderland DD862, which was damaged in an attack on the U-Boat U672, on the 24th April 1944. Enquiry was made from John Picken, a grandson. Flight Lieutenant Fellows married Aileen Bridget Grant, who was born in Swanlinbar, Co. Cavan.

Fl. Sgt. Charles Albert Mark Barber, RAAF. A Sunderland DW106, was lost off the coast of Portugal on the 17th December 1943, while on way from Pembroke Dock to West Africa. Thought to have been shot down by German planes. There were 19 persons on board, including the crew. An enquiry from Mrs.Senta-Anne Koy, Australia, a relation. One of the crew, Sgt. Samuel Hughes, had trained at Killadeas.

There were enquiries from other people about crashes in Ireland that were not connected to the Donegal Corridor; some could not be answered due to no information being available. Most of the above people had little or no information on how their loved ones died, until they got details from history available in Fermanagh. To have assisted so many families (66) in helping them to learn what happened, has been very fulfilling. There are many more somewhere, who, one day, might look for information.

We shall remember them, those who flew beyond the storm, into the sunset and never returned. They shall not grow old, as we that are left grow old. Age shall not weary them, nor do the years condemn them. At the going down of the sun, and in the morning, we will remember them.

U.S. airmen in the R.C.A.F

Special mention must be made of the 7,000 airmen from the United States of America, who served in the Royal Canadian Air Force, in the early years of World War 2. They will be known as our "American Patriots – Canadian Warriors". They flew, and fought, with their Canadian comrades in the RCAF, with over 700 of them killed in action. After much research, Halifax 57 Rescue, (Canada), has found all their names, and the home towns of those Americans who paid the ultimate price for freedom. All 48 States of the then United States of America, are represented on this R.C.A.F. 'Roll of Honour', with at least one son killed-in-action from every state.

The majority of these 700 plus are not listed on their State Memorials. During this project, we will give special tribute to these unknown Americans and heroes, who flew and died for Canada in the R.C.A.F.

It is the least we can do for our best friends and neighbours.

The following piece is taken from the publication "SHORT BURSTS", the Canadian Air Force newsletter.

Irish Nationals in the R.C.A.F.

This master list of Irish names is courtesy of Martin Gleeson and Chris Charland, sourced from Bill Chorley's RAF Bomber Command Losses series, supplemented by other sources. All are shown in the Flight Engineers position, in a Halifax crew as per Chorley. Unfortunately, all died. There are certainly more from experience to date.

Sgt. M.J. O'Donovan, Killed in Action (K.I.A.) 8/9-10-'43, 427 Sq., Halifax LK900, RCAF, from Rosscarbery Co. Cork.

P/O. J. Gilliard, K.I.F.A. 15/16-2-4, 432 SQ. RCAF, Halifax LK761, from Killester, Co. Dublin.

K.I.F.A. = Killed in Flying Accident.

Sgt. P. Furlong, K.I.A. 30/31-3-'44, 425 Sq. RCAF, Halifax LW429, from Killincarrig, County Wicklow.

Sgt. J.K. McMahon, K.I.F.A. 29/30-8-'44, 434 Sq. RCAF, Halifax MZ626, from Limerick City. Sgt. James McMahon was one, out of at least fifteen, Limerick-born aircrew, who died in WW2, while serving in RAF Bomber Command.

Sgt. R.L. Dinnen, K.I.F.A. 5/6-3-'45, 420 Sq. RCAF, Halifax NA190, from Ballyjamesduff, Co. Cavan.

Sgt. J.K. Gilvary, M.I.A. 17/18-8-'43, 419 Sq. RCAF, Halifax JD458, Air Bomber, from Bray, Co. Wicklow. M.I.A. = Missing In Action.

Sgt. W.P. Maher, K.I.A. 23/24-9-'43, 419 Sq. RCAF, Halifax JD457, Air Bomber, from Clonmel, Co. Tipperary.

Sgt. H.B. Hill, K.I.A. 20/21-1-'44, 434 Sq. RCAF, Halifax LL135, Air Gunner, from Ballycanew, Co. Wexford.

P/O A.C. Middleton, K.I.A. 25/26-2-'44, 427 Sq. RCAF, Halifax LK759,

Air Gunner, from Dublin

F/O R.R. Irvine, K.I.F.A. 5/6-6-'44, 426 Sq. RCAF, Halifax LW382, Air Bomber, from Dublin.

The following are noted as being from Northern Ireland.

Sgt. R.W.S. McNally, K.I.A. 23/24-9-'43, 419 Sq. RCAF, Halifax JD457, Wireless Operator, from Lisburn, Co. Antrim).

P/O. J.C. Harris, K.I.A. 2/3-2-45, 428 Sq., Lancaster KB792, Flight Engineer, from Belfast, Co. Antrim.

****

My memories of many brave young men that I never knew, have come forward from the misty past, where they had remained secure for three score years and more. They have come at a time when most needed. Similar mists shrouded many Irish hill tops, and kept them hidden from those brave young airmen, who died so tragically when their planes collided with them. From mountain tops all over Ireland, their bodies were removed, with dignity and respect, looked on with sadness by the local people, who knew that they were some mothers sons.

Bodies of recovered crew men were transported, in several cases for hundreds of miles, by an Irish Army that was 'of the war period, but not in the war'. Placed into the care of their comrades, at Belleek and other border crossings, some to be returned to their home land and families; others, laid to rest in the Irvinestown War Graves, with many of their comrades who met a similar fate. Graves there have been tended with loving care by local residents, who never knew the men, yet they cared for them as they would for their own brothers. Special attention is given to the graves for Remembrance Day, on 11th November each year, when fresh Poppy crosses are placed on them. As they cared for them, their thoughts turned to the many more air crews who were lost at sea; they never returned, and have no known graves. They are not forgotten; their names are recorded locally on a "Roll of Honour" of the 330 who died while serving at Lough Erne.

In recent years, I have stood by the graves, with wives, brothers, sisters, sons, daughters and grandchildren, who, for the first time in over 60 years, could grieve at the grave of a loved one. They had learned how they died; a final chapter has been written for them, and it brought peace to so many. The families have a special place in the hearts of the people of Fermanagh, and other places in Ireland, who have ensured that their loved ones will be remembered for all time.

On the lonely mountains, valleys and moor lands of Ireland, there are memorial stones on crash sites, with the names of the men engraved on them, placed there by local people.

CHAPTER 11

Crashes at Lough Erne, The Donegal Corridor and in Ireland

A number of crashes happened in Ireland, or off its shores, during the Second World War. Two hundred are recorded in Eire, neutral Ireland, including forty in Co. Donegal alone, and about twenty four German air craft, mainly in the southern part of the island. A number of Lough Erne based flying boats were lost in the Atlantic, having either failed to return from missions, or were shot down by U-Boats. Many American planes being ferried across the Atlantic never reached their intended destination in Britain; there is no record of those losses.

Catalina AM265 from Lough Erne crashed on Aunagh Hill, Glenade, Co. Leitrim on 21St March 1941. All eight crew were killed.

British Saro Lerwick Seaplane. Not a crash, this plane landed in Bundoran Bay on 10th April 1941, as it was low in fuel. The crew were entertained at Finner Camp while fuel was brought by lorry from Castle Archdale.

Catalina AH532 failed to return from an Atlantic patrol on 21St April 1941.

Catalina AH536 crashed near Gay Island, Lough Erne, on 7th May 1941. Ten crew died. Nine still on board. This is a recognised war grave.

Catalina Z2153 crashed in Lough Erne, on 3rd December 1941.

Catalina W8148 Lough Erne based crashed, on 23rd December 1941, at Pembroke Dock, Wales.

Catalina Z2148 Lough Erne based crashed at Sullen Voe, Shetlands, on 19th January 1942. Seven died.

Catalina AH535 failed to return from patrol on 17th May 1942.

Catalina AH545 failed to return from an Atlantic patrol, on 15th July 1942. This Catalina had spotted the Bismarck on 26th May 1941.

A Catalina landed on Lough Gill, Co. Sligo, low in fuel, on November 17th 1942. Fuel was brought from Castle Archdale, and the plane took-off and returned to base.

Catalina FP 127 Foundered in The Irish Sea, 20th December 1942. No casualties.

Catalina FP239 crashed on 30th December 1942, at Reaghan Hill, Omagh, Co. Tyrone. All crew killed.

Catalina FP184 Lough Erne based crashed on 30th December 1942, at Kilwhannel Hill, Ballantrea, Scotland. Two died.

Catalina FP194 crashed on Lough Erne on 10th May 1943.

Catalina FP110 crashed on 24th May 1943, near Innismackill Island, Lough Erne. One died.

Catalina W8414 crashed on Lough Erne 26th May 1943. No casualties.

Catalina FP155 crashed on 10th July 1943, in the sea off North Donegal coast. Crew rescued by British Navy boat.

Catalina FP114 missing, 3rd August 1943, on ferry flight Castle Archdale to Gibraltar.

Catalina FP101 crashed 7th August 1943, near Duress Point Lough Erne. Two died.

Catalina AH551 crashed on 16th October 1943, at Whitehill, Ballinamallard. All crew killed.

Catalina FP120 crashed on 2nd November 1943, near Rockall off Donegal coast. All crew died.

Catalina W8408 ran aground, Lough Erne, 8th November 1943. No casualties.

Catalina FP240 failed to return from Atlantic patrol on 22nd November 1943. All crew lost.

Catalina FP193 hit the water in a dive near Boa Island, Lough Erne, on the 9th January 1944. Seven died.

Catalina Z2147 damaged landing at Killadeas on 9th January 1944. No casualties.

Catalina AM266 struck Buoy on Lough Erne, 3rd March 1944. No casualties.

Catalina AH541 crashed near Montgomery Rock, Lough Erne on 17th April 1944. Three died.

Catalina JX576 wrecked on Rocks, Killadeas, on 20th July 1944.

Catalina FP203 damaged on landing, Lough Erne, 16th August 1944. No casualties.

Catalina Z2152 damaged on landing Lough Erne, 20th August 1944. No casualties.

Catalina JX242 crashed on 20th November 1944, at Lough an Laban, Churchill, near Lough Erne. Eight died.

Catalina JX252 crashed on 26th November 1944, at Ely Lodge, Enniskillen. Nine died.

Catalina JX208 crashed on 19th December 1944, at Castlegregory, Tralee, Co. Kerry. Nine died.

Sunderland W3988 crashed on 3rd December 1941, at Doonbeg, Co. Clare. Nine died, two crew members were saved.

Sunderland W3998 crashed on 22nd December 1941, at Mount Batten. Lough Erne based. Eleven died.

Sunderland W3977 crashed in Donegal Bay on 6th February 1942. Twelve died.

Sunderland W 4025 shot down by 'Friendly' convoy fire on 31st July 1942. Eleven died.

Sunderland W4000 blown up on the 1st August 1942 by own depth charges, after ditching near convoy. Eleven died.

Sunderland W4001 struck rock Lough Erne on 4th October 1942. No casualties.

Sunderland W3995 ran aground Lough Erne 10th January 1943. No casualties.

Sunderland W6075 hit sand bank on Lough Neagh on 12th May 1943. No casualties.

Sunderland DD846 crashed off Clare Island, Co. Mayo, on 25th May 1943. Eleven died.

Sunderland DD857 crashed on 30th June 1943 landing on Lough Erne. Two died.

Sunderland DD859 shot down on 4th August 1943, by U-boat U489 near Iceland. Four died.

Sunderland DD848 crashed on 22nd August 1943, Mt. Brandon, Co. Kerry.

Eight died.

Sunderland JM712 damaged by U-Boat U-470, on 17th October 1943. Four died.

Sunderland DD861 ditched in the Bay of Biscay, 3rd September 1943. No casualties.

Sunderland W6030 ditched near Iceland, 28th September 1943. No casualties.

Sunderland DD858 split hull landing on Lough Neagh, on 23rd October 1943. No casualties.

Sunderland DP181 bow split open on landing on Lough Erne, 11th November 1943. Five died.

Sunderland DD863 lost on 13th November 1943, off Donegal coast. Twelve died.

Sunderland W4036 crashed on 18th November 1943, at Maghoo Point, L. Erne. Three died.

Sunderland W6031 sunk by U-Boat U-648, on 20th November 1943. Eleven died.

Sunderland W6013 crashed on Knockalyd Mountain, Co. Antrim on 5th December 1943. Nine died.

Sunderland DW110 crashed on Blue Stack Mountains, Donegal on 31st January 1944. Seven died.

Sunderland W6028 crashed Trory Hill, Enniskillen on 20th February 1944. Two died.

Sunderland W6008 ditched at sea on 12th March 1944. Sunk by British Navy. No casualties.

Sunderland DV990 shot down by U-Boat U- 921, on 24th May 1944. Twelve died.

Sunderland ML760 shot down by U-boat, in the Bay of Biscay on 12th June 1944. Twelve died.

Sunderland NJ175 crashed on 12th August 1944, at Corlea / Cashelard, near Belleek. Three died.

Sunderland ML823 crashed off Bloody Foreland, Donegal on 6th September 1944. Nine died. Crew member W/O R.H. Voyce survived.

Sunderland DV978 ran aground Lough Erne on 4th December 1944. No casualties.

Sunderland ML883 sank at moorings, Calshot on 17th December 1944. Had been based on Lough Erne. No casualties.

Sunderland NJ183 crashed at Knocknagor, Irvinestown on 11th February 1945. Eleven died.

Sunderland ML743 crashed on mountain near Killybegs, Donegal, on 14th March 1945. Twelve died.

Sunderland NJ184 ran aground at Lough Erne on 8th May 1945.

Sunderland EJ 157 engine fire at Castle Archdale on 12th May 1945.

Sunderland W4003 damaged in storm at Killadeas on 21st September 1945. Sunderland PP113 dived into sea, 20m North of Inishtrahull Island, on the 5th July 1947.

Sunderland SZ574 struck obstruction at Lough Erne, on 31st May 1948.

Lerwick L7267 crashed on 10th September, 1942. No casualties.

Mosquito HJ887 engine failed on take-off, at St. Angleo, on 27th June 1944.

Martinet HP133 crashed near Crannagh, Omagh. on 15th March 1943. Two died.

Martinet HP731 crashed in Knockatallon, near Scotstown, Co. Monaghan, on 28th November 1943. One died.

Martinet HP980 taxied into truck at St. Angelo on 4th March 1944.

Martinet HP 70 crashed at Cassie Bawn, Mullaghmore on 17th December 1944. No casualties.

Martinet HP351 engine fire at St. Angelo on 12th April 1945.

Pinace boat sank in Lough Erne on 14th October 1942. Ten died.

Land plane crashes associated with Donegal Corridor, or crew members buried in Irvinestown.
Lockheed Hudson FH223 crashed in the sea near Sligo on the 23rd May 1942. The pilot is buried in Irvinestown.

Flying Fortress B-17 landed on Mullaghmore Beach on 5th December 1942. A new engine was brought and fitted. The plane took off again, on 22nd December 1942.

Flying Fortress B-17 crash landed at Athenry, Co. Galway on January 15th 1943. Sixteen persons were on board, including very high ranking American Officers, who were brought to Belleek by the Irish army. This story is in the book 'Eagles Over Ireland' by Paul Browne.

Flying Fortress B-17 landed on Tullan Strand, Bundoran on 10th May 1943. No casualties.

Halifax EB134 crashed at Tuam, County Galway on the 7th November 1943. Seven died. Four crew members are buried in Irvinestown.

Flying Fortress Boeing B-17 crashed on Tuskmore Mountain, Co. Sligo, on 9th December 1943. Three died.

Flying Fortress Boeing B-17 crashed at the Graan Monastery, Enniskillen, on 9th December 1943. Seven died.

Halifax LK704 crashed at Rougey Cliff, Bundoran, Co. Donegal on 23rd January 1944. Eight crew members died, three are buried in Irvinestown.

Flying Fortress B-17 crash landed at Fintragh, Killybegs, Co. Donegal on the 20th February 1944. No casualties.

Liberator B-24 crashed at Abbeylands, Ballyshannon, Co. Donegal on 19th June 1944. Two died.

Halifax MZ980 ditched in Mullaghmore Bay on the 9th February 1945. Two crew members died, one is buried in Irvinestown.

A total of fifty three air craft that either landed, crash landed, or force landed, were returned to the Allies. Some were simply refuelled; others repaired and took off again for base. A number were salvaged, and the wreckage returned across the border.

Counties Carlow, Longford, and Westmeath, were the only counties where no World War Two planes crashed.

Patrols to protect convoys coming from Africa, and ships from Gibraltar, were particularly at risk, as at least twenty five Sunderland's were lost in the Bay of Biscay.

On 7th December 1944, a Sunderland from Castle Archdale landed on Lough Melvin, low in fuel. As this was not a crash, and as Lough Melvin is partly in Eire, and partly in N. Ireland, it is not included in the website of Dennis Burke. I was told about this incident by Seamus McGowan of Kinlough, who remembers seeing the Sunderland on the lake. He remembered the date, 8th December. This was a church holiday, and a day off school, so they were free to watch the plane take off. The incident was confirmed by John J. Treacy, who was a pupil in Garrison school. He clearly remembered the plane taking off, and flying low over the village. While the Flying Boat was on the lake near Garrison, waiting on fuel to come from Castle Archdale, it had enough fuel to keep one engine running. Local business people, and the police, thought it would be good to bring some food and other refreshments out to the crew. But every time a boat got near the plane, it moved away. Someone then had the brilliant idea to place a car on the shore, and sent a Morse code message to the plane, using the car headlights. This worked very well, and so the goods were delivered to the crew. When the fuel arrived, and was got out to the Sunderland, it taxied over to the Kinlough end of the Melvin, to gain the full advantage for the take-off.

U-boats sunk or damaged by Lough Erne based Flying Boats
U-753 sunk on 13th May 1943.

U-229 damaged on 17th May 1943.

U-518 damaged on 27th May 1943.

U-440 sunk on 31st May 1943.

U-489 sunk on 4th August 1943.

U-610 sunk on 8th October 1943.

U-470 damaged on 16th October 1943.

U-625 sunk on 10th March 1944.

U-672 damaged on 24th April 1944.

U-921 damaged on 24th May 1944.

U-246 sunk on 30th April 1945.

German aircraft crashes in Ireland in World War 2.
A number of German reconnaissance flights took place over Ireland in the early stages of the war. They are known to have photographed Belfast, and other places, including Lough Erne. Then of course there was the blitz of Belfast on several occasions and the number of bombs dropped in Dublin, and

other parts of the south east of neutral Ireland. Only one German plane came down above a line from Galway to Meath. Once Germany had taken over France it was a reasonably short flight to bomb any part of Ireland.

German planes regularly dropped mines in Belfast Lough, and off the east coast of Northern Ireland. On 24th July 1940, a German four engine Focke-Wulf 200C Condor, left Brest airfield in Brittany, France, on a mining mission to Belfast Lough. The pilot was Hauptman Volkmar Zenker, with four other crew members. There were four mines on board, and when the release mechanism was activated, only three of the mines dropped into the Lough. Zenker made a turn to drop the last mine; his he did at a low level, but when the throttle levers were advanced, both port engines failed to respond, with the result that the plane crashed into the sea. Zenker and two of the crew were able to launch a rubber dinghy, but the other two crew members went down with the plane. Zenker and his comrades were picked up from the sea, and brought to Larne, and then interned.

On the 20th August 1940, a Focke-Wulf FW200, crashed on Mount Brandon, Co. Kerry.

On the 15th September 1940, a Dornier sea plane crashed into the sea off the South coast, Wexford.

On the 29th September 1940, a Heinkel crashed into the sea off the Wexford coast. Five died.

On the 1st October 1940, a Focke-Wulf FW200, crashed into the sea near Castletownbere, Co. Cork.

On the 11th October 1940, a Dornier crashed into the sea off the Meath coast. Four died.

On the 22nd October 1940, a Focke-Wulf FW 00 crashed at Clifden, off the Galway coast. Six bodies were recovered.

On the 22nd October 1940, a Focke-Wulf FW200 crashed off the Kerry coast.

On the 18th November 1940, a Blohm und Voss crashed off the Irish coast. Five died.

On the 25th November 1940, a Blohm und Voss crashed off the Blasket Island, Co. Kerry. Five crew members were interned.

On the 5th February 1941, a Focke-Wulf crashed on Cashelane Hill, a Cork mountain. Five died. One crew member survived.

On the 23rd February 1941, a Heinkel HE111, crashed into Kenmare Bay, off the Kerry coast. Four died.

On the 3rd March 1941, a Focke-Wulf crashed near Dingle, Co. Kerry.

On the 3rd March 1941, a Heinkel HE111 crashed at Tacumshane, Co. Wexford.

On the 5th March 1941, a Heinkel HE111 crashed on Skellig Rock, Co. Kerry. Four died.

On the 1st April 1941, a Heinkel HE 111 crashed at Ballyristeen, Co. Waterford. Five interned.

On the 8th April 1941, a Heinkel crashed into Irish Sea.

On the 18th April 1941, a Focke-Wulf crashed near Schull, Co. Cork. Six interned.

On the 6th May 1941, a Heinkel crashed in Wexford. Two crew members died, two survived.

On the 10th June 1941, a Heinkel crashed at Nethertown, Carne, in Wexford. Five died.

On the 26th August 1941, a Junkers JU88 crashed in Belgooly, Co. Cork. Four interned.

On the 11th October 1941, a Heinkel HE111 crashed at Kilteady, Wexford. Four died.

On the 27th December 1941, a Junkers JU88 crashed at Mastergehy, Waterville, Co. Kerry. Four interned.

On the 3rd March 1942, a Junkers JU88 crashed at Mount Gabriel, near Schull, Co Cork. Four died.

On the 21st March 1942, a Heinkel HE111 crashed in Kerry. Four interned.

On the 27th June 1942, a Junkers JU88 crashed off Hook Head, near Wexford. Four died.

On the 23rd August 1942, a Junkers JU88 crashed at Tramore, Co. Waterford. Four interned.

On the 23rd July 1943, a Junkers JU88 crashed at Dursey, in Cork. Four died.

On the 13th December 1943, a Focke-Wulf FW200 crashed at Dromineer, near Neenagh, Co. Tipperary. Eight were interned.

On the 5th May 1945, a Junkers JU88 landed in Meath. Three were interned.

Germany had plans prepared for the invasion of Ireland in the early stages of the war. **Operation Green,** for the invasion of neutral Ireland, was to take place at the same time as **Operation Sea Lord,** the plan to invade the south coast of England. **Plan Kathleen,** was the name given for a plan to invade Northern Ireland. The old bridge at Belleek was mined by the Irish army, to be blown up in case of an invasion.

CHAPTER 12

Lost at sea with no known graves

Out of the kindness of our hearts, let us remember the large number of brave young men who failed to return from missions over the Atlantic. They have no known graves; they share the ocean bed with the many thousands of Irish people, who died in Coffin Ships in famine times, and were buried at sea. Let us remember the many thousands lost in battle ships and convoy vessels, during WW2.

Catalina AH532 failed to return to base, on the 21st April 1941.
Fl. Lt. Henry Francis Dempster Breese   W/O Clifford Bond
Sgt. Walter Henry Balch   Sgt. Alexander Vaughan McRae
A/C Herbert Vernon Norton   A/C James Frank Woodard
Sgt. Horace Arthur Tann   F/Sgt. Alfred Tizzard
Fl. Sgt. Leslie Stewart Dilnutt

Catalina AH545 failed to return to base, on the 15th July 1942. This plane had spotted the Bismarck on 26th May 1941.
Sq. Leader Lawrence George Becham   P/O Adrian Fennel
F/Sgt. James Edward Bacon   F/Sgt. Sydney Leslie Beamont
F/Sgt. Reginald Clayton Graham   F/Sgt. John Nevil Tew
Sgt. Peter Bray   Sgt. Christopher William Cooke
Sgt. Albert Henry Thomas Davies   Sgt. William Roy Norley

Catalina FP114 missing on Ferry flight to Gibraltar, on the 3rd August 1943.
Sgt. G.W. Farler   Sgt. R.J. Howell
Sgt. E.E. Matty D.F.M.   Sgt. R. E. Newman
Sgt. R.O.S. Selwyn   F/Sgt. D.S. Summers

Sgt. L.M. Trimmer   Sgt. A. Whitman

Catalina FP120 crashed off the Donegal coast, on the 2nd November 1943.
F/O Kenneth Hipwell   Sgt. Harold Edwin Scarman   Sgt. Peter Phillip Bacon
Sgt. Cyril Barraclough   Sgt. James Male   Sgt. Charles Edward Poots
Sgt. Albert Upton   F/Lt. Edward Earle Muffitt F/O Douglas Haig Dianey

Catalina FP240 crashed at sea on 22nd November 1943.
P/O Francis Peter Graves   Sgt. Robert Anderson
Sgt. Edwin Alfred Dennis Barnes   Sgt. Earl Darragh Morrison
Sgt. Alexander Fordyce Sutherland   Sgt. Allan Douglas Warder
Sgt. John Glynne Williams   Sgt. Owen Douglas Hodgkison
Sgt. John George Ley

Sunderland W3988 crashed at Doonbeg, Co. Clare, on 3rd December 1941.
Sgt. E.W. Jackson   P/O E.G. Marker
LAC A.P. Walker   P/O. W.S. Emmet, New Zealand

Sunderland W3977 crashed in Donegal Bay, inward bound to Lough Erne.
F/Lt. Francis W. Smith   P/O John P. Bartlett
P/O Rodney W. Smith   F/O Henry Kilchen
F/Sgt. Harold S. Mason   F/Sgt. Norman Clare
Sgt. John F.C. Smith   Sgt. Arnold Rolfe
Sgt. Hugh Jones   Sgt. Kenneth Nutt
Sgt. Gordon W. C. Jacobson   A/C Eric Hopkinson

Sunderland W4025 Shot down on 31st July 1942, by 'Friendly' convoy fire.
F/Lt. James Robert Trail   F/Lt. Walter Harry Wakefield
P/O John Allen   F/Sgt. James Andrew Collins
F/Sgt. Maurice John Tomley   Sgt. William Bluck
Sgt. John Robert Goodings   Sgt. Harry Scarce
Sgt. Norman Williams   Sgt. Clifford Gurnet Fort
Sgt. Vivian Lewis

Sunderland W4000 blew up on the 1st August 1942, by own depth charges, after ditching near Convoy WS21.
F/Lt. Leonard Cox   P/O Arthur Alfred Webster
P/O Robert William Wilkins F/Sgt. Harold Abbott
F/Sgt. Leonard Battersby   Sgt. Arthur Corfield Somerset Clive-Davies
Sgt. Frank Henry William Gurnett   Sgt. Donald Kenyon
Sgt. William Jack Mansbridge   Sgt. George Falconer Muir
Sgt. Phillip Ralph Field

Sunderland DD846 crashed off Clare Island, Co. Mayo on the 25th May 1943.
W/O Wallace R. Thompson   Sgt. David Purvis
Sgt. James Hird   Sgt. John Rowe

Sunderland DD859 shot down by U-boat U-489 near Iceland, on the 4th August 1943.
P/O Harry Bertram Parliament   Sgt. Herbert Gossop
F/Sgt. Frank Hadscroft   W/O John Stanley Kelly

Sunderland DD863 lost off the Donegal coast, on the 13th November 1943
F/Lt. A.F. Brazenor   F/Sgt. S.G. Brockway
F/Sgt. R.J. Money   Sgt. H.W. Fell
Sgt. H.E.E. Attwood   Sgt. M. F. Flynn
Sgt. D. Bigmore   Sgt. L. Morgan
F/Sgt. R.W. Stiff   P/O R.H. Wilson
F/O H.B. Pharis

Sunderland W6031 sunk by U-boat U-648 on the 20th November 1943.
F/Sgt. Bruce Goulden Burton   F/Sgt. Robert Aird Park
Sgt. Norman Percival Cook   Sgt. Ronald Montague Fisher
Sgt. Noel Neil Lewis   Sgt. Walter McKay
F/O Charles Gordon Gorrie   F/O Wilfred Sydney Johnston
F/O Robert Harry Strauss   F/O Jan David Butler Ulrichsen
F/Sgt. Norman Barrett

Sunderland DV990 shot down on the 24th May 1944, by U-Boat U-921

Sgt. P.D. Andrew	Sgt. D.J. Harvey
F/O G.B. Gingell	F/Sgt. L.W. Guggiari
F/Lt. Edgar W. Beattie	W/O James C. Burke
W/O Keith M.G. Fleming	F/O Thomas E. Frair
F/O George E. Holley	P/O John H. Hamilton
Sgt. John C. Seeley	P/O Claude Senton

Sunderland ML760 shot down by U-boat in Bay of Biscay, on 12th June 1944. Based at Pembroke Dock, this Sunderland had been at Castle Archdale.

SQ. Leader W.D.B. Ruth	F/O C.J. Griffith
F/Sgt. J.C.L. Humphrey	F/Sgt. J. W. Hobson
F/O P.A.C. Hunt	F/Sgt. D.J.M. Currie
Sgt. D.E. South	F/Sgt. D. Sharland
F/O A.V. Philip	F/Sgt. F. Foster
Sgt. J.R. French	F/Sgt. Edwin Watson

Sunderland ML823 crashed on 6th September 1944, off Bloody Foreland, Co. Donegal.

F/O Frederick W. Greenwood	F/O Edwin E. McCann
F/L George F. Cornwall	F/O Herbert S. Seibold
W/O Joseph A.D. Dore	Sgt. Lawrence Quinn
F/O Liddle	Sgt. Anderson
Sgt. Canton	

Halifax LK 704 crashed on 23rd January 1944, at Rougey Cliff, Bundoran, County Donegal.

P/O Norman Glyn Gzowski   F/O Clarence Scott

Lockheed Ventura crashed on the 27th August 1942, in Sligo Bay.

P/O Charles Candonnel Findlay   Sgt. RHYS Maelgwyn

Whitley P5045 crashed in Galway Bay, on 12th March 1941.

P/O Edward D. Deer   P/O William H. Edwards
Sgt. Stanley Donald Sutherland Goodlet

****

Two Years in the Water

There are two graves in the Church of Ireland Cemetery, Irvinestown, inscribed **"Known only to God."** There rest the two unidentified bodies recovered from Lough Erne.

R.A.F. Officer's body found in Lough Erne

At 8:30 am, on Monday morning, (August 1946 ?) while out in a boat in Lower Lough Erne, Thomas Muldoon of Kesh, saw, lying in six inches of water, at the shore off Gay Island, the naked body of a man. The head was missing, as were also the two arms from the elbows down, and the right leg, from the shin bone down. The body was naked except for a shoe and sock on the left foot.

Muldoon reported the matter at Kesh R.U.C. Barracks, and Sergeant Bentley immediately went to the scene, with a constable, some R.A.F. Officers, and an R.A.F. doctor. They found the body in a very advanced state of decomposition, and the doctor was of the opinion that the body had been in the water for over a year at least.

The body was brought ashore, and on Monday evening, an inquest was held by Dr. McBrien, Deputy Coroner. Serg, Bentley, and the R.A.F. medical officer from Killadeas, having given evidence, a verdict was returned that the cause of death was drowning.

It is believed that the body is that of an R.A.F. officer, killed in one of the plane crashes during the war. The black shoe is thought to be an officer's shoe.

Catalina FP183, of 131 OUT, hit the water in a dive, near Boa Island, on 9th January 1944. Missing after the crash were Sgt. Harry Bagley, aged 21, and Sgt. Edward Le Roy Gross, aged 19. In grave number 84 is "An air man of '39 –'45 war.

An Officer of the R.A.F, buried on the 28th August 1946, " KNOWN UNTO GOD"

Apart from the known war graves, these are the only men missing in crashes on Lough Erne.

The other air man "Known unto God" was buried on 9th December 1943, in grave 41.

CHAPTER 13

Short Bursts

Former RCAF member John Moyles, and his wife Doreene, have been editing the periodical "Short Bursts" since the late 1980's. They have published many stories relating to the members of the RCAF who served with Coastal Command, and in doing so have kept former comrades in contact with each other, over the years. John and his wife emigrated from Ireland to Canada in 1927. They came from Dangan's Farm, Mount Mellick, Queen's County, in the Irish midlands. Of course, that is in the Irish Free State, and the County name has been changed to its original name, County Laois. This chapter contains a number of short stories, and is dedicated to John and Doreene, in appreciation of the great work they have done over the years.

Censorship in the Irish Free State during World War 2
When researchers went to past editions of Irish newspapers, they could find nothing about World War 2 air crashes, or other incidents, that happened in the country. There was a very strict form of censorship imposed in the state. Newspapers and radio stations were forbidden to report on any incidents where either the Allies or Axis forces were involved. The large number of air craft crashes throughout the country went unpublished. There were many reasons for this, mainly political, but generally, not to make public the fact that the neutral state was giving strong support to the Allied countries. As far as possible, this was to keep any word of this assistance from reaching the Germans.

Many allied aircraft were classified as being on non-belligerent flights, such as weather or air - sea rescue exercises. Crews of such air craft were not interned, but were returned across the border to re-join their units. The crews of aircraft that were engaged in war exercises were interned in the Curragh Camp, in Co. Kildare. This included the crews of German planes, forced to come down in the Free State. As a result, the locally published "Donegal Democrat" was forbidden to publish a report on the U.S. Liberator that crashed near the town. This was only one of many major news worthy happenings to occur, practically on the Democrats front door. What makes the story all the more intriguing, was the fact that a leading London daily newspaper carried the story, giving the Liberator crash at least five column inches. It detailed the excellent work done at the scene by the Irish Army, the Garda, the L.D.F., the area medics, and local people, all who gave aid to the injured and survivors.

It was to be in June 2005, that a memorial service to the two young American airmen, who lost their lives in the Liberator crash of June 19th 1944, was held, and that a framed citation was presented to the Sheil Hospital, in recognition of the medical assistance given to the men injured in the area, in World War 2 plane crashes.

During the years of World War Two, 1939 to 1945, a number of air craft crashed in this district. A number of crew men died, and many more suffered serious injuries The injured were treated with care and affection, by the staff of the Sheil Hospital.

The Sheil Hospital

The dead were, with respect and dignity, prepared for the return to their home lands. Surgeons Patrick Daly and James Gordon, Sister Fedelma, the Matron, Sisters of Mercy, and lay nurses, treated many young air men in this hospital.

On 19th June 1944, an American Liberator aircraft crashed at Abbeylands, near the home of Nurse Maureen Kelly, S.R.N., who, with members of the Red Cross, the Local Defence Force, the Gardai, and the Irish military, assisted at the scene. There they carried out their duties under most dangerous conditions, with burning wreckage and exploding ammunition, without any consideration for their own safety.

Two members of the crew, Corporal Riley W. Cannon, and Sergeant Carlos F. Maestas, died in the Sheil as a result of their injuries. The eight survivors received all necessary medical attention.

On 12th August 1944, Sunderland Flying Boat NJ175 crashed at Cashelard / Corlea . Three crew men died at the scene. Pilot Fl. Lt. E.C. Devine; F/O. R.T. Wilkinson; and Fl. Sgt. Jack Forrest. Nine crew members survived the crash; several of the injured suffered severe burns and broken bones. Following treatment at the Sheil Hospital, the nine survived. All were members of the Royal Canadian Air Force.

On 10th of August 2002, one of the survivors, Sergeant Charles Singer, on his first visit back to Ireland since that fateful day, called to the Sheil Hospital to meet the staff, and thank them for the medical treatment that he got here in 1944. He had no doubt, but that the care and the attention given to him by the staff here saved his life.

Sunderland NJ175 had taken off from Castle Archdale that morning, to patrol the Atlantic Ocean. The Liberator was on a ferry flight from Goose bay, Newfoundland, to St. Angelo Air Port, Enniskillen, when it developed engine trouble, and force landed in Abbeylands. A local committee organised a memorial stone engraved with the names of the crew, to be placed on the crash site.

****

Gods Acre

In Esquimalt, British Columbia, there is a veteran's cemetery known as Gods Acre. It is an honoured final resting place for the many members of the Canadian services who died during both world wars, and other conflicts. More than 2,500 B.C. military personnel, and their family members, are buried at God's acre.

In Memory of the Air Crews

Canadians from a far off land
Extended to us a helping hand
Catalina's set forth in the dead of night
Valiant men off to the fight.

For freedom and the defence of you and I
True heroes of land and sky
Sunderland's too, along the Donegal Corridor fly
Mighty thunder of the engines, through clouds high.

Called to arms to go and serve
With great courage and great nerve
What must have been a wonderful sight
In the early mist of morning light!

Ooh! What stories you could tell
As you flew into the jaws of hell
For some there will be no return
And those with regret we will mourn.

These men so generous gave their all
In answer to this national call
Who are now fleeting spirits passing through
Blessed by deeds they did do.

Crew and comrades in eternal sleep
At rest in Lough Erne waters deep
Who now await the trumpets roar
And will reply to the flag once more.

This memorial in your name
Enshrined in our hearts you will remain
So soft rain keeps green the fern
Another day dawns over the Lough of Erne.

Poem by Helene Turner placed at the Lough Navar memorial stones by an unknown kind person.

The Flying Boats of Lough Erne

I still lie here, beneath the hill
Abandoned now, to natures will
My hangers down; gone – my people all
The only sound; a wild bird's call.

But my mighty "birds" shall rise no more
I do not hear the engines roar
And never now does my bosom feel
The lift of that silver keel.

From this ageless hill their voices cast
Thunderous echoes of the past
And still in lonely memory
Their great broad wings sweep down to me.

Laughter, sorrow, hope and pain
I shall never know these things again
Emotions that I came to know
Of strange young men, so long ago.

Who knows as evening shadows meet
Are they with me still? That phantom fleet!
And do their ghosts still fly unseen?
Across my waters so wide and green.

And in the future should the forest tall
Change my face beyond recall
I shall still remember them
My metal birds and long dead men.

My trees grown high: obscure the sky
O! Remember me when you pass by
For atop these curling waves
I was you home in other days.

Women at war

Not enough attention has been given to the part played by women in World War 2. During the Second World War, the role of women in Canadian society changed dramatically. Canada needed women to pitch in and support the war effort from their homes, to work at jobs that were traditionally held by men, and to serve in the military. Canada had its own version of 'Rosie the Riveter', the symbolic working woman who worked shoulder to shoulder with men in factories, on air fields, and on farms. They proved that they had the ability, skills, and strength to do the work the men did. Their smaller physical size and manual dexterity helped them develop a great reputation for fine precision work in electronics, optics, and instrument assembly. Canada's Elsie Gregory McGill was the first woman in the world to graduate as an aeronautical engineer. She worked for Fairchild Aircraft Limited during the war. In 1940, her team's design and production methods were turning out more than 100 Hurricane combat aircraft each month. In 1941-'42, the Canadian military was forever changed, as it created its own women's forces. More than 50,000 women served in the armed forces during the Second World War, many of them overseas.

In Britain there was the much appreciated ladies 'Land Army', who did a great amount of farm work including driving tractors to crop and harvest land produce. Many WAAF's, as the women's branch of the RAF was known by, served on Lough Erne. The story of one of them, Doreen Bastik, is in the 'Donegal Corridor' book. I corresponded with Doreen for about 6 years, until she passed away about 2008. The first WAAF's arrived in Castle Archdale in November 1942. They played a most important part in the 'Battle of the Atlantic', in Coastal Command. Being in 'Signals', the ladies kept the daily records in the Operations Room of all flights from the base, and would have known by name the crews of the flying boats. They would have been the first to know when a plane was overdue, and when one would fail to return to base. When this happened, they shared the same grief as the men's comrades. As well as being in 'Signal's, a title that included many trades, they acted as drivers of both cars and large trucks.

In June 2000, Breege McCusker was the principal local organiser for a visit to Castle Archdale, for the members of 422 Squadron Association; most of them had travelled from Canada for the event. Included in the guests were three members of the WAAF who had served at Castle Archdale. One of them, Lynne Powell, recalled how she had worked in flying control at St. Angelo and Killadeas. She was the first WAAF at St. Angelo, and remembered the Americans coming to Fermanagh. They had a very different radio system to the RAF one, and the girls were always waiting to get nylon stockings from them. During her visit, she returned to the old control tower at St. Angelo, and recalled many of her experiences at radio control in those days. Joining Lynne for the visit, were Phil Stone and Pat Hamilton, two of her comrades from the old days at Lough Erne.

At an early stage in the war, the women were trained as pilots, and were responsible for flying fighter aircraft from the factories to bases all over England, in all kinds of weather. A number of them lost their lives in crashes, due mainly to bad visibility, fog, and storm. At a later stage in the war, they were trained to deliver larger planes, such as Halifax and Lancaster's, to big air bases. They were to prove to be excellent pilots of the big planes, as not one of them ever had a crash, or lost a big bomber. A number of the lady pilots were awarded medals for bravery, courage, and exceptional service during the war. The story of the lady air women is told in a book "THE WAAF" by Squadron Leader Beryl E. Escott, a native of Newfoundland.

The first Irish woman to qualify as a pilot was Lady Mary Heath. (1896-1939) Born Sophie C.T.M. Pierce-Evans, in Knockaderry, Co. Limerick. She died in London in 1939, as a result of a fall from a tram. She was reared in the home of her grandfather by two maiden Aunts, who discouraged her passion for sports. She took a degree in science at the Royal College, Dublin. Before training to be a pilot, she served as a Dispatch Rider in England and France, during World War 1. In 1926, she became the first woman to hold a commercial flying licence in Britain, and the first to parachute from a plane. She was the first pilot to fly a small open cockpit plane from Capetown to London, a journey that took from January to May 1928. Had she not died at an early age, she would have become a pilot in the RAF.

CHAPTER 14

A Selection of stories and events

The return visits of two Canadian Squadrons, Squadrons 422 and 423, have been well received here in Co. Fermanagh. These visits are well documented in Breege McCuskers book "Fermanagh and Castle Archdale in World War 2". On several occasions, members of 422 Squadron held reunions at Castle Archdale, and attended memorial services at crash sites, where engraved stones that had been erected by Gary Pentland and his team of helpers, were unveiled. In May 2005, a group of Canadians came to Fermanagh, to take part in V.E. day celebrations. This proved to be a poignant experience for them. One of the party's members was Dom Soucie, whose uncle, Warrant Officer Jean Marie Soucie, of Canadian Squadron 423, lost his life in the air crash of Sunderland NJ183, at Knocknagor near Irvinestown, on the 11th February 1945.

Over 60 years on, Dom took the opportunity to visit the crash site, and to see the memorial stone, inscribed with the names of all the crew members (11) who died in the crash. The stone had been prepared and erected by Irvinestown historian, Breege McCusker, and her helpers, sometime before the visit. The Sunderland had just taken off from Castle Archdale when it crashed, and on the crew was F.O. Terence R. Hailstone. Some years after the crash, local man John McFarlane, Enniskillen, visited the site, and found a bracelet belonging to Terence Hailstone. After intensive research, John traced the family of F/O Hailstone in Canada, and returned the bracelet to them. Leaving the memorial stone, the group of 9 Canadians went to the war graves in Irvinestown, and placed wreaths on the graves of the crew who were buried there. They then went to the RAF museum in Castle Archdale, where they presented the staff with two paintings, one, of the main building as it had been during the war, and another of a Sunderland taking off from Lough Erne. They also presented the uniform of the then Commanding Officer, Group Captain Costello of 423 Squadron, to the museum.

The next connection with 423 Squadron came in June 2010, from John Picken, World War 2 historian in Barrie, Ontario, Canada. His grandfather, F/Lt. F.G. Fellows, had served with the Squadron at Castle Archdale. John sent me details of a new hanger that was erected at the Head Quarters of 423 Squadron, in Canada. A letter was sent to John from Lieutenant-Colonel Jeff Tasseron, Commanding Officer, 423 Maritime Helicopter Squadron, St. John's, Newfoundland.

Dear Mr. Picken,

It gives me great personal satisfaction to inform you, that, owing in no small part to the excellent historical effort you made with your website, and to the kind efforts of A/CAS staff, and my Wing Commander, I have succeeded in gaining approval to officially name the new 423 Squadron Hanger "Archdale Hanger". An important space within the building is to be formally associated with your Grandfather - F/Lt. F.G. Fellows.

In closing, thank you again for your work in commemorating the early history of 423 Squadron, and for the care and compassion with which you have made the historical records of Castle Archdale access able on line.

Warmest regards,
Jeff Tasseron.

The next connection with 423 Squadron came in April 2011, when 20 members of the modern Squadron came on a visit to Castle Archdale, where the old World War 2 Squadron had served with Coastal Command. They were the helicopter crew that operated from the Canadian Frigate HMCS St. John, which was on a NATO exercise in Europe. The ship was in Belfast for several days, and the 423 men came on a visit to Castle Archdale. Captain Robin Izzard and his comrades, were welcomed by Breege McCusker to Co. Fermanagh. She gave them a detailed history of the Flying Boat base, and took them on a guided tour of the grounds, where their former comrades had served over 60 years ago. The party then stopped off at the War Graves, in the Church of Ireland cemetery, where a number of 423 air men lie at rest in well-tended graves. A number of local people were also present to welcome the men to the town. At an enjoyable lunch in Mahon's Hotel hosted by the Canadians, gifts were exchanged between the guests and hosts. In a letter of appreciation from Captain Robin Izzard, he said;

"I want to express many thanks from myself and our entire Air Detachment, for taking the time to talk and share stories with us, and the added surprise of the books on the 'Donegal Corridor' given to each of the men. The day was more than we ever could have imagined. It had a deep physical, and emotional impact on all of us. Give our thanks to all involved who made us so welcome.

I cannot express what an honour it was to have met, and shared, the day with people who share and are so committed to preserving our history. It was truly an unforgettable day.

Sincerely, Robin Izzard, Captain. 423 (MH) Sqn., HMCS St. John's Air Det.

The Bismarck: What is not commonly known, is that there were two Lough Erne Catalina's involved in the Bismarck episode. The first one, Catalina AH545, spotted the mighty German battle ship, on the 26th May 1941. It kept the ship under observation, until it had to return to base when it had only enough fuel left to complete that flight. Catalina FP240 took over the tracking of the Bismarck, and guided the British battle ships to it. During the course of this, task Catalina FP240 was subject to intense flak from the anti-aircraft guns on the German ship, and suffered severe damage to its hull. The Catalina remained at its post until the British ships took over, and commenced the battle that ended with the sinking of the great ship. In the early part of its voyage in the North Atlantic, the Bismarck had been found by a Spitfire, but it soon disappeared in the ocean fog. It was a Swordfish plane from one of the warships that launched a torpedo, which struck the rudder of the Bismarck, and damaged it so severely that the ship could only move in large circles. Almost 2,000 German sailors died on board, and only about twenty were saved. This is many more than died in the sinking of the Titanic in 1912.

In spite of the damage it suffered, Catalina FP240 made its way back safely to Lough Erne. Here it was in danger of sinking at its moorings, with water getting into it from the damage to the hull. An urgent message was sent to the Auxiliary Fire Service in Enniskillen, which had been provided with a trailer fire pump that could be towed by a private car. Two members of the fire service took the pump, by boat, to where the Catalina was moored near its base. They kept the water pumped out until temporary repairs were made to the holes in the hull; this enabled the flying boat to take off, and be flown to a place where it could be hauled up on a slip way, for permanent repairs to be done to its hull.

Sad to say, Catalina AH545 failed to return from an Atlantic patrol, on the 15th July 1942, and Catalina FP240 crashed at sea on the 22nd November 1943, with the loss of its crew.

There were some plane crashes in Ireland that were not directly connected to the Donegal Corridor. A good example is the crash of Halifax EB134, which crashed at Lavally, near Tuam, Co. Galway, on the 7th November 1943. The seven crew were killed, and four of them were buried in Irvinestown, Co. Fermanagh. Fl. Lt C.H. Sansome; Fl. Sgt. A.S. Johnston; Fl. Sgt. A.J. Gallagher; - all members of the Royal Australian Air Force -, and W/O Norman W. Gardener, of the Royal Canadian Air Force.

The fate of Halifax EB134 remained part of the folklore of the Tuam area for 63 years, when local historian, Mrs. Anne Tierney, on hearing some stories of the crash, decided to do some research on the event. Her search led her to George Smith, resident of Jersey Island. George in turn referred Anne to me, and from there on, the project developed beyond any hopes she may have had. After the exchange of many e-mails and phone calls, I eventually met with Anne in Knock, Co. Mayo, when I had to drive some friends there. It was a short drive for her from Tuam. We went over many of the details of the Halifax crash which enabled her to prepare a story for the Tuam 2006 annual journal "JOTS". Her story was suitably titled "The Sound of Wings". The following year, 2007, she came to Belleek, and I brought her to the graves in Irvinestown of the young men who were buried there. For her, it was a most emotional and moving experience, to stand at the graves of the men whose names had become so familiar to her, and part of her life.

Having seen some of the memorials on crash sites in Fermanagh and Donegal, Mrs. Tierney decided that the site of the Halifax crash should have a suitable memorial near where it happened. Ably assisted by local teacher Tony McHugh, a committee supported by the Town council, and various other local groups, the work commenced. The research was not confined to speaking to the now limited number of locals who remembered the incident; soon it took a national flavour that developed into an international one, reaching to Britain, Australia, Canada, and the U.S.A., as Anne traced the relations of the crew. In the book "Halifax EB134 Memorial", researched and compiled by Anne Tierney, the full story of the erection of the memorial garden is recorded.

It can be said without fear of contradiction that nowhere on these islands is there a memorial to compare with the one planned and erected by the people of Tuam and Lavelly. It could be well described as a Garden of Remembrance. Nor was there ever such a distinguished gathering of guests from all over the world, including relations of a number of the dead crew men. The co-operation between town and country is a prime example of what can be achieved, when Irish people decide to honour seven young airmen, strangers to the country, who died here in 1943. The men did not have a choice as to where they would die, but if they had had a choice, they would have wanted to spend their last moments with the people of Galway. The site for the magnificent Garden of Remembrance was donated by a local land owner, materials were given by suppliers, and labour was voluntary.

Amongst the distinguished guests present for the ceremony on Sunday, 5th August 2007, was Her Excellency Anne Plunkett, Australian Ambassador to Ireland; The Minister of State for Overseas Assistance; Michael Kitt, Assistant Defence Attaché at the British Embassy in Dublin; RAF Warrant Officer Brian Mahoney; Mission Administrative Officer of the Embassy of Canada; Mr. John Banin; RAF Group Captain David Stubbs OBE, Aldergrove, N. Ireland; The Mayor of Tuam; the Chairman of Galway Co. Council; elected members of the national and local government; Church leaders; senior Gardai officers; Irish Army Officers; members of the local F.C.A.; and army veterans, who had served with distinction with the United Nations. The Irish Air Force honoured the occasion with a fly past of modern planes. The Royal Australian Air Force was represented by a young lady, Squadron Leader Emily Cameron. After the ceremony, refreshments were served by the ladies in nearby Lavally school. Quite an achievement, this, for about 300 guests.

Halifax RG843   Four Halifax planes crashed in neutral Ireland during World War 2: EB134 in Tuam; LK704 at Bundoran, County Donegal; LL145 in County Cork; and MZ980 ditched in Mullaghmore Bay, County Sligo. A fifth Halifax, which was not connected to the Donegal Corridor, crashed on Achill Island, on the 16th June 1950, long after the war was over. Its story is not so well known, and I think that it should be recorded here.

Halifax RG843 of RAF 202 Squadron was based at Aldergrove, Co Antrim. It was used for meteorological surveys, and was on a routine Met. Flight over the Atlantic, when, with its crew of eight, it failed to return to base on 16th June 1950. The last message from the plane said that it was near the Shannon estuary, had completed its mission, and was returning to base. When the alarm was raised two Lancaster's, and another Halifax, took off from the base and conducted an intensive search off the west coast of Ireland. Nothing was found. Michael Fadian was tending sheep on Croghaun Mountain, Achill Island, Co. Mayo, which was covered in dense fog, when, at about 4-30 in the evening, he heard the noise of aircraft engines, followed by a loud explosion. When the fog eventually lifted, Michael, using binoculars, saw a rubber dinghy, and other items, on the mountainside. Going to the scene, he found four bodies. He immediately hastened down the mountain to report the matter to the Gardai at Keel. A large search party, including Gardai, a doctor, a clergyman, and local people, was organised and set off up the mountain. The bodies of the crew were recovered from the mountainside and the wreckage, and taken on stretchers to Keel. Their names were: - F/O Ernest George Hopgood; F/O Joseph Kevin Brown; Fl. Eng. Harold Shaw; Lac James C. Lister; F/O Michael William Horsley; W/OP Cornelius Joseph Rogan; W/OP Bernard Francis de Sales McKenna; and A/G Martin Gilmartin. The bodies of the eight young men were returned to their comrades in Aldergrove.

****

The Flying Fortress at Athenry, Co. Galway I first learned about the crash of a Flying Fortress B-17 in Co. Galway in 2002, when an e-mail was re-directed to me from Paul Browne of Athenry. I think he had sent it to someone in Fermanagh, more in hope than anticipation; during his research into the crash, he discovered a connection with Belleek. I made contact with Paul, and offered to help him in any way possible. He had, for over 12 years been researching the event, and as the 60th anniversary of the crash was fast approaching, it was decided to set up a committee to mark the occasion. Paul sought the assistance of Finbarr O'Regan, who joined the committee. I suggested that he contact Breege McCusker of Irvinestown, the historian with a lot of knowledge on the World War 2 history. The next step was when Paul and Finbarr travelled to Belleek; collected me, and we went to Irvinestown to meet with Breege. It was a most interesting afternoon, and with Breege's knowledge of the history of World War 2, the Belleek Connection with the Athenry Flying Fortress was discovered. Paul and Finbarr returned to Galway, very happy with their worthwhile trip to Fermanagh. Paul was now in a position to include this part of the story in his book "Eagles Over Ireland".

At 2am on Friday the 15th January 1943, the Flying Fortress 'Stinky', left Gibraltar in good weather conditions, bound for Portwreath, Cornwall, England. During the flight, the aircraft missed an important turning position over the Bay of Biscay. It also lost radio contact with the RAF. The plane was first seen over Athenry on the morning of the 15th of January. It circled around looking for a suitable field large enough to land on; many fields had been spiked to prevent belligerent aircraft from landing, in the event of Ireland being invaded. This had been a strong possibility in the early years of the war. The pilot also wanted to burn up as much fuel as possible, to lessen the danger of fire when landing. *(This makes one wonder how capable navigators were, for, in this case, as in the case of the Doonbeg Sunderland, there was as much fuel used searching for a place to make an emergency landing, as would have brought them to Fermanagh)* Eventually, the pilot choose a large field near the Agricultural College, and it was here that the B-17 landed, at 11:50, almost ten hours after leaving Gibraltar.

While the plane did suffer considerable damage, there were no injuries to the occupants. Amongst those on board were several very high ranking American officers:- Lieutenant General Jacob Loucks Deveres; Major General Edward Hale Brooks; Brigadier General Gladeon Marcus Barnes; Brigadier General Williston Birkhimer Palmer; and Colonel William Thaddeus Sexton, of the U.S. Army.

The crew were:- Major Earle Lynn Hormell; Captain Thomas M. Hulings, Pilot; Lieutenant James Kemp McLaughlin, co-pilot; Lieutenant C.B. Collins, Navigator; Sergeant Blanchard; Sergeant Tippen; Sergeant Johnnie J. Tucker; Sergeant L. Harris; Technical Sergeant Laurence E. Dennis; and Technical Sergeant E.D. Parrish, all US Army Air Force. Sergeant R. Boland, an English RAF Pilot, was also on board.

Once members of the 1st Battalion of the Western Command of the Irish army arrived on the scene, the site was secured, and under the Command of Major James Timoney, C.O., Renmore Barracks, Galway. A guard was placed at the B-17, and the men brought into Athenry. There they were taken into the Railway Hotel, which was a fine establishment, enabling the unexpected guests to clean up, relax, and enjoy a much needed hot lunch. The meal for 21 people was paid for by General Divers, at a cost of £4 4s 0d.

Contact was made with the Irish Government, and the U.S. Embassy in Dublin. Due to strict censorship, no report on the incident appeared in the papers. Arrangements were made by the Irish Army to provide transport for the journey to the Royal Ulster Constabulary Police Station, at Belleek, Co. Fermanagh. The party set off from Athenry at 8pm, on the night of January 15th, 1943. It took several cars, and an army truck containing all the baggage, to bring everything to Belleek. At 2am in the morning, they crossed the bridge over the River Erne at Belleek, where they were taken care of by Head Constable John Briggs. Mrs. Briggs welcomed the group into her home, and made them tea, coffee, and other "stimulant beverages. Soon they were joined by Colonel Goodwiley, Major McLoughlin, and Lieutenant Smith, from the American Headquarters in Lurgan. Once again the "Donegal Corridor" was put to good use by the Allied forces. All salvageable parts and equipment was removed from the B-17, and returned across the border.

****

About 50 years after Sunderland DD846 crashed off Clare Island, Co. Mayo, Gary Pentland from Gortin, Co Tyrone, prepared a memorial stone with an engraved plaque, with the names of the crew on it. He transported the stone all the way to Clare Island, and had it placed there in memory of the crew. Seven of the bodies including, that of F/O Ernest Paige, D.F.C. of the RCAF, were recovered, but four were lost at sea. They were W/O W.R. Thompson; Sgt. D. Purvis; Sgt. J. Herd; and Sgt. J. Rowe.

In October 1996, Robert Paige, his wife, Audrey, from Ontario, Canada, and sister Nancy, from California, came to Clare Island for the unveiling of the memorial stone. A local musician played a lament in honour of Ernest and his comrades. All the Paige family knew was that Ernest had lost his life during the war, and it took this visit to Ireland for them to learn the full story. The family had also visited the graves of their brother and his comrades in Irvinestown. Tony Kearns, from Dublin, an expert on World War 2 plane crashes, explained that the Sunderland was operating from Lough Erne, Co. Fermanagh, protecting shipping convoys from the dreaded U-Boats.

On February 5th 1943, a number of American fighter planes were being ferried to North Africa. Due to adverse weather conditions in the Bay of Biscay, several of them were forced to return to base in England. One of the planes a Bell P-39h-! (Be Air Cobra of the USAAF), piloted by 2nd Lt. Charles M. Kirshiner, got lost in the bad weather, and made a forced landing at Campsie, Co. Wexford, Ireland. One of the first people to arrive on the scene was an Irish army medical doctor, Captain Kernan. Seeing the army officer in uniform, Lt. Kirschiner assumed that he was to be arrested. This was not part of Dr. Kernans duties, and both men sat on the wing of the plane enjoying a smoke, and a chat, while the authorities dealt with the crash. The air craft was later salvaged by the military, and by the 12th March, was taken to the border, and passed over to the authorities there in Northern Ireland. Dr. Tom Kernan, one of the local doctors in Belleek, is a son of the above mentioned Dr. Kernan.

****

Sgt. James McEvoy was a member of the crew of Sunderland ML743, of 201 squadron, which crashed on Crownarad Mountain, Killybegs, Co. Donegal, Ireland, at 02.15 hours, on Wednesday, the 14th March 1945, when returning to Lough Erne from an Atlantic patrol. There were no survivors of the crash, and it was the last plane from Castle Archdale to crash on the Donegal Corridor.

Recently, on 19th September 2010, a grandniece of Sgt. James McEvoy, Helen McGlone, who lives in Scotland, got in contact with me. As a result of the information I gave to Helen, and of her own research into the death of her Granduncle, she uncovered the following story. James' body was recovered from the wreckage, and he was buried in the family plot in Glasgow.

"I found some wonderful information about James after you gave me pointers. He was, in fact, on a plane that sunk a U-boat. It was the U-boats first outing, and in later years divers found its wreckage somewhere off the coast of Scotland, and went down to investigate and photograph the wreck. The family of the wife of the U-boat Commander sent a decorative little silver token, which the divers placed on the boat for her.

I found the story of the dive expedition in old BBC news records, and James's sister was enthralled by the story. She said her mother managed to have James's body returned home for burial. The story of the U-boat sinking was, I thought, quite touching. All hands on board died of course. It was a war when so many young men, still children really, not so different from our own young men, if different at all, lost their lives. Helen's grandmother later told her, that after hearing all the stories about the crash and the U-boat, that what she now knew about James's story, information they were never given at the time, and never knew, made her feel closer to him than she has ever felt before, and she is 85 years of age.

WE REMEMBER THEM

In the rising of the sun and its going down – we remember them
In the blowing of the wind and in the chill of winter – we remember them
In the opening of the buds and in the warmth of summer – we remember them

In the rustling of leaves and the beauty of autumn – we remember them
In the beginning of the year and when it ends – we remember them
When we are weary and in need of strength – we remember them

When we are lost and sick at heart – we remember them
When we have joys we yearn to share – we remember them
So long as we live, they too shall live.
We remember them!

For now they are now a part of us, as we remember them.

CHAPTER 15

Crash memorials and letters of apprectaion

Catalina FP239 One of the early Catalina crashes was that of Catalina FP239, that happened on Reaghan Hill, near Omagh, Co. Tyrone, on the 30th December 1942, in a severe snow storm. All of the crew died:- Sgt. William Nichol; LAC Leslie Greenhalagh; Sgt. Arthur Horton Perkins; Sgt. Daniel Ward Yates; Sgt. Frederick Herbert Hilling; Sgt. John Edward Slade; Sgt. Charles Bernard Ridge; Captain John Samuel Orr; (a native of Pomeroy, Co. Tyrone), F/O Matthew James Hall Newma;. (all RAF), Sgt. George Wilson Lowther, RAAF; and F/O Robert Mercer Adams, RCAF.

Gary Pentland, Gortin, and Jim McLaughlin, Omagh, were the principal men responsible for the erection of the memorial stone on the crash site. In recent years, the original stone was enhanced by the extension of the area, concrete flags placed around it, and white posts and chain surround, makes it a worthy memorial to the young men who died here. Jim has been a regular contributor to the *'The Catalina News'* journal, and keeps them up dated on anything about Catalina's based on Lough Erne.

Catalina AH551 The crash of Catalina AH551 at Whitehill, near Ballinamallard, on the 16th of August 1943, was another one where Gary Pentland and Jim McLaughlin were involved in playing an important part in this memorial, as was Seamus Gormley of Whitehill, who had erected a temporary memorial at the site in the mid 1980's. The crew who died in the crash were: Squadron Leader Patrick George Cooper, RAF; F/O David Leigh Sproule, RCAF; F/O Frank Herbert Grainger, RCAF; Sgt. John Harvey Hodgson, RCAF; Sgt. James Millard Allen, RCAF; Sgt. Valentine Hinton Louis, RCAF; W/O Gerald Frederick Hardy, RAF; and F/Sgt. Donald Mudd,

RAF. There were two survivors who were badly injured. The memorial service was held on the 22nd May 2003. The stone used was once a base for an old water-driven mill wheel, and is about a ton in weight.

The introduction was by F/Lt. Jack Logan, RCAF, and the plaque was unveiled by LAC Wes Maxwell, and Fl/Lt. Peter Moffatt, both of 422 Squadron. Peter had travelled all the way from Australia to be present. The Dedication and Benediction was by Canon V. McKeon, Ballycassidy. The parade Commander was Squadron Leader Harry Kerrison, RCAF, who also recited the Act of Remembrance. Andrew Gordon, from Churchill, gave a rendition of "The Last Post and the Reveille"; Pipe Major Kenneth Ferguson played the Lament 'Flowers of the Forest'. The late Noel Ingram of Ballycassidy, supplied the Canadian 'Maple Leaf' and RCAF ensigns for the 422 Colour Party. He arranged for the attendance of local clergy, a bugler, and a piper, and erected traffic signs. Noel, and his wife Barbara, were also deeply involved in arranging the reception, which was held in Trory Parish Hall, after the Whitehill ceremony. Thanks were expressed to the land owners, Basil and Matthew Dunne, for permitting the memorial to be placed on their property. Sadly, Noel was to pass away in 2010.

Sunderland W6028 Shortly after taking off from Lough Erne on the 19th February 1944, Sunderland W6028 crashed on Trory Hill, Enniskillen. Two of the crew were killed in the accident: P/O/ Leslie A. Hebenton, RCAF, and Sgt. R.W. Bodsworth, RAF. Civilians living nearby rescued injured crew from the wreckage. On Wednesday, the 31st May 2000, as part of the program for the re-union of 422 Squadron Association, a Memorial and Dedication Ceremony was held at the Air Crash Site, Trory, Enniskillen.

The introduction was by Alan Cathcart, and the memorial installed by Gary Pentland and friends, was unveiled by F/Sgt. Syd Irving, (crash survivor) and F/Lt. Bernard (Bud) Crooks. (crew member). The dedication was by Canon V. McKeon, Ballycassidy. The Last Post and Reveille was played by Christopher McClelland.

The Act of Remembrance was by Squadron Leader Stan Nichols, and the Benediction by Canon V. McKeon. The Parade Commander was Squadron Leader. Harry Kerrison, chairman of the 422 Squadron Association. The Colour Party was F/O Charles (Chuck) Turnbull, 422 Association;. Squadron Leader Harry (Tiny) Wrenshall, 422 Association; and Sgt. Pat Donnelly, Omagh Branch RAFA.

Catalina JX252, crashed at Drumcose, Ely Lodge, Enniskillen on the 26th November 1944. This was the last Catalina to crash in Co. Fermanagh. It crashed on a hill overlooking Lough Erne, during a snow storm, when returning in the early hours of the morning from an overnight anti-U-boat patrol in the Atlantic. The blue memorial stone was donated by Hadden Quarries, Carrickmore, Co. Tyrone. Transported by Jack Mulligan to the home of Jim McLaughlin, Glenhordial, Omagh, where it was cut and prepared by Gary Pentland, and Jim McLaughlin. This was one of ten memorials planned and erected by Gary Pentland, and his helpers. Three are in Co. Fermanagh, three in Co. Donegal, three in Co.Tyrone, and one in faraway Clare Island, Co. Mayo, in the west of Ireland. Six are for Sunderland's, three for Catalina's, and one for a Hurricane.

The crew of JX252 were: Sgt. John Rew; F/Sgt. Noel George Edward Ladbrook; Sgt. David Henry Pidgeon; Sgt. James Pringle; Sgt. Edmond Thomas Crow; Sgt. Bernard Alfred Rosentreter; W/O Reginald William Shallis; Sgt. Alfred Sonenthal; and Sgt. Kenneth Percy West.

After a selection of sacred Marches played by the Magheraboy Flute Band, David Scott, on whose land the crash had happened, and who had organised the ceremony, gave an introduction to those present. There then followed a selection of readings from scripture; by Cyril Rosenberg; who was deputising the Rabbi Abraham Citron; of the Belfast Jewish Community; and by Precentor Brian Courtney, Rector of St. Macartens Cathedral, Enniskillen. The Jewish Ex-Servicemen's Association was represented by 90 year old Herbert Humphreys, Ex-RAF.

The unveiling of the memorial was performed by Joyce Hotston, fiancée of the Captain, W/O Reg Shallis, and David Ladbrook, nephew of Fl. Sgt. Noel Ladbrook. The memorial was dedicated by Cyril Rosenberg, and Precentor Courtney. The Last Post was by Andrew Gordon, of the Churchill Silver Band. The Dedication was by Paul McGettigan, RAFA, Enniskillen. The Reveille was performed by Andrew Gordon, and the Lament, "Flowers of the Forest", by Jonathan Watson. A poem entitled "The Flying Boats of Lough Erne" was read by Dorothy Scott. A laying of a wreath was performed by Joyce Hotston. An Appreciation was given by David Ladbrook, and the conclusion, by David Scott. The National Anthems were performed by Magheraboy Flute Band.

The Colour Party was; William Gault, Enniskillen Branch, RAFA; Pat Donnolly, Omagh Branch, RAFA; Herbert Humphreys, Association of Jewish

Ex- Servicemen; Gordon Johnston, and Sabrina Brown, Enniskillen Branch of the Royal British Legion.

The Abbeylands, Ballyshannon, Liberator Crash. On Monday the 19th June 1944, an American Liberator B-24, made a crash landing at Abbeylands, Ballyshannon, Co. Donegal, shortly after 9 pm. It was one of the few crashes that happened in day light, and was witnessed by many people. The B-24 was on a ferry flight from America to Nutts Corner airbase, on the shore of Lough Neagh, Co. Antrim. In the early hours of the morning, the plane took-off from Goose Bay, Newfoundland. The pilot was 2nd Lt. Arthur H. Dittmer, and he had a crew of nine U.S. airmen. As ferry aircraft approached the west coast of Ireland, they had two points of contact, one was their own U.S. Radio station at Magheramena, near Belleek, the other was the RAF radio station at Dernacross, south west of Belleek. Also, near the Look-out Posts on the coast, were the large letters EIRE, painted in white to let the airmen know that they were safely across the Atlantic.

After eleven hours flying, the pilot realised that, due to strong head winds, he would not have enough fuel to take him to Nutts Corner, and so he was diverted to St. Angelo air field, in Enniskillen, County Fermanagh. When he got to St. Angelo, the air field was closed by fog and low cloud. He turned back towards the coast again, and selected a large field to crash land the Liberator. It was badly wrecked on landing, and sadly, two of the crew were killed, and four injured. In 2005, the Ballyshannon Historic group decided that the crash should be marked with an engraved memorial stone, near the site.

A Memorial and Dedication Ceremony was arranged to take place in Colaiste Cholmcille, the large college in Ballyshannon, on Sunday the 19th June 2005, the 61st anniversary of the crash. Mr. Carl Duggan, Historic Ballyshannon, was M.C., and the large number of guests was addressed by Mr. Jim Slevin, Chairman of Donegal Local Development Company. The stone was unveiled by Mr. Jon Benton, Deputy Chief of Mission (acting U.S. Ambassador) United States Embassy, Dublin, and Commandant Sean Curran, 28th Infantry Battalion, Irish Army Camp, Finner, Ballyshannon. Also in attendance were Defence Attaché Paul Flynn, and Sergeant Major Don Doherty, of the U.S. Embassy. The American National Anthem was played by the Ballyshannon Brass and Reid band. A selection of appropriate scripture readings were read by representatives of the four local churches. The last

Post, and Reveille, was played by an army piper from Finner Camp. Mr. P.J. Branley, Chairman of Historic Ballyshannon, gave the final address. An acknowledgement was read by Mr. Peter Daly, whose father was a surgeon in the Sheil Hospital, and who attended to the injured crew members. An appreciation was read by Mr. Jon Benton, Deputy Chief of Mission. (Acting U.S. Ambassador) The ceremony was attended by Government Ministers. and other public representatives. Many guests had travelled from Northern Ireland for this historic event. which concluded with the playing of the Irish National Anthem. All present were treated to refreshments before departing for home.

Plaques on bridges over the River Erne at Ballyshannon and Belleek

On Wednesday the 18th April 2007, a long standing ambition of two Fermanagh historians, Breege McCusker of Irvinestown, and Joe O'Loughlin of Belleek, who specialise in the World War 2 period, finally came to pass. On that day, in two moving ceremonies, matching plaques were unveiled on the bridges that cross the River Erne, at Ballyshannon and Belleek. These plaques record the fact, that this was the famous World War 2 Donegal Corridor flight path, over the section of neutral Irish territory from Belleek to Ballyshannon, plus three miles of territorial water into the Atlantic Ocean. The flight path enabled Catalina and Sunderland Flying Boats from Lough Erne, to give protection to shipping convoys, bringing much needed supplies across the Atlantic; the convoys quite often contained Irish ships. While all Allied ships were under strict orders not to go to the rescue of the crews of torpedoed vessels, the Irish ships ignored this order, and during the course of the war rescued over 700 British merchant seamen from the Atlantic.

The plans for the Donegal Corridor plaques entailed a considerable amount of quiet diplomatic negotiations, before the event was finalised. Involved were the Ballyshannon Town Council, Donegal County Council, Fermanagh District Council, their officials, and all political parties. The Ballyshannon ceremony was presided over by Mayor John Meehan, local historian. Anthony Begley acted as Master of Ceremonies. The plaque was unveiled by local man Sean Slevin, who over 60 years ago, as a member of the Local Defence Force, assisted in rescuing the injured from plane crashes in the area, and their removal on stretchers, as well as handling the bodies of those who died. These tasks had to be carried out on the most difficult of terrain, sometimes at night, down mountain sides, for long distances, to the nearest roads. The Ballyshannon Brass and Reed Silver Band, under the musical direction of Mr. Michael Gallagher, provided suitable music at both venues, and at the end of the Belleek ceremony, sounded the Last Post, and Reveille, in memory of those who flew westwards into the setting sun, but never returned to see another sunrise on Lough Erne. A large number of local people attended the events, and recalled memories of seeing the aircraft in the skies many years ago.

All present then travelled to Belleek, where Breege McCusker acted as M.C., and John O'Kane, Chairman of Fermanagh District Council, presided for the unveiling, which was carried out by local man Frank Garvin, ex-RAF, who had flown in Lancaster's over Europe, as a radio operator. Both ceremonies were televised for U.T.V. by the popular Paul Clark, and for RTE by Eileen Magneir. Everything had to be done to a strict time table to accommodate an RAF air/sea helicopter, that circled around Belleek Bridge, and flew along the Donegal Corridor. As the ceremony concluded a small flying boat, based at St. Angelo, did a fly past along the River Erne. At both venues, suitable passages from the scriptures were read, by Clergymen from the local churches.

A little known fact is that the old bridge at Belleek had been mined in the early stages of World War 2, by the Irish army, in case of an invasion of the country by Germany. I remember seeing the Irish army carrying out the work when on my way to school.

Gifts were exchanged between pupils from the local schools at the end of the ceremony, and then all present were treated to refreshments, provided by Belleek Pottery. Representing the staff of Fermanagh District Council was Mr. Robert Gibson, Director of Leisure, Tourism and Arts. Representing Donegal County Council was the County Manager, Mr. Michael McAloone; and Mrs Mary Daly, Town Clerk, represented Ballyshannon Town Council. Mr. Brian Pendry, Chairman of the Fermanagh Flying Boat Association, was also present, as was Mr Gary Pentland, who, with his team of helpers, had placed suitable memorial stones on at least twelve crash sites, one as far away as Clare Island, in Co. Mayo, where a Castle Archdale Sunderland had crashed in 1943, with loss of life. Breege McCusker and Joe O'Loughlin have placed memorial stones on another ten or more crash sites, in Fermanagh and Donegal.

Sean Slevin and Frank Garvin were delighted to have been invited to perform the unveiling of the plaques, as were their families. Sad to say, both men died about a year after the event, and the two of them are buried within about 50 yards of each other, in St. Patrick's cemetery, Belleek.

****

A selection of letters of appreciation from families

Calgary, Alberta, Canada

June 26th, 2000

Dear Friends,

Thank you for the kindness you showed to Louise and myself during our visit to Ireland. We could never have managed without you. I am enclosing the names of the Canadians that were on the plane that crashed at Bundoran. (Halifax LX704) I hope this will be of help. One of them, Clarence Lorrie Scott, was in the back part of the plane that went into the ocean and was never found. This is from the air force book that I have with all the men's names that were killed or missing during the war. I hope this will help to clear up the matter.

Thank you for everything, it was wonderful to meet with you. I hope you will be able to erect the memorial on the beach. I talked to Louise the other night and she is working on getting some financial aid. We are both interested. Thanks again, my best to you all.

Sincerely,

Mayo Murphy, Formerly wife of Freddie Dawson.

****

North Vancouver, B.C., Canada
18th August 2000

Dear friends,

As I advised you before, the Canadian Government would not participate in this memorial stone that you would like to put up on the beach. They feel that as they have placed headstones on the graves of the men who died, their duties have been carried out. So I went to the children of my siblings, and Mayo, and her son by Fred Dawson. They are all very pleased with the plan, and together we can subscribe $400.00 which we hope will contribute to the cost.

Would you be so kind as to send me the exact copy of the engraving that will be on the stone, so we can check that the names are accurate. If we can come back for the dedication of the stone, it should be around the spring.

Regards to all from Louise Williams. (Sister of Vladimir Adamic)

****

Canadian Embassy, St. Stephen's Green, Dublin

April 30th 2002

Dear Mr. O'Loughlin,

Thank you for your letter of April 29th, 2002, informing the Canadian Embassy about the Memorial and Dedication Ceremony in Bundoran, Co. Donegal, of a memorial stone being erected in memory of the crew of a Halifax aircraft which crashed in 1944.

We congratulate you and Mrs. McCusker on this initiative, and have brought your letter to the attention of Col. Michel Legault, Air Force Adviser, at the Canadian High Commission in London. The Canadian Defence Liaison Staff in London are responsible for military matters in Ireland. As a result, we would hope to have a Canadian Department of Foreign Affairs or Department of National Defence presence at the ceremony on September 12th.

Yours sincerely,

Bill Gusen,

Charge D'affaires, a.i.

****

Canadian Embassy, St.
Stephen's, Green, Dublin

August 14th 2002

Dear Sir,
Further to your letter of April 29th and our reply of April 30th, 2002, the Canadian Defence Liaison Staff at the Canadian High Commission in London are inquiring if we had and further news about the Memorial and Dedication Ceremony on September 12th in Bundoran, Co. Donegal. The Liaison Staff are planning to send a Canadian Forces representative and are anxious for more details of the event.

Would be grateful if you would contact me so, I may pass on any information. Thank you.

Yours sincerely

Janet C. Green,
Attaché.

****

Canadian Defence Liaison Staff,
London

19th September 2002

Dear Joe,
Congratulations, the events surrounding the remembrance moments in Irvinestown and the dedication ceremony at Bundoran last Thursday were truly a fitting tribute to the memory of our valiant airmen. I was particularly impressed by the support you gathered from the local communities. Your hard

work, stamina and personal relationship were of great importance. Please, pass on my appreciation on behalf of the Canadian Air Force to all those who participated.

As you did mention, Breege McCusker played a crucial part in the project. I have passed on my appreciation to her under separate cover. I include a copy of the notes I used at the dedication ceremony. In return, I would welcome a copy of the very touching words you passed on at the beginning of the presentations at the dinner that evening. The dinner, which combined great company, delicious food and a warm atmosphere, was the perfect conclusion to a most successful day. I will follow up on the original copy of the letter to the Archbishop, a rather important historical document indeed.

In closing, my thanks to all concerned for making me a part of a very special day. I salute all as true friends of Canada. I have been touched in a way that I will remember for ever.

Sincerely Michel Legault, Colonel. Air Force Advisor.

Steelstown Road, Derry.

13th August 2002.

Dear Joe,

Just a little note to thank you for inviting me to yesterday's ceremony. I enjoyed it very much.

I was delighted to meet Chuck. He is a very nice man. Congratulations to yourself and Breege on such a successful and fruitful piece of research.

Wishing you God's Blessing,

Yours sincerely,
Edward Daly,
Retired Bishop of Derry.

Bishop Edward Daly was present, as a young boy, at the crash of Sunderland NJ175, when Chuck survived it.

****

Calgary, Alberta, Canada

November 16th 2002

Dear Joe,

I would like to thank you for the wonderful hospitality, kindness and good company during the visit to Ireland with my mother. The dedication ceremony was far beyond our expectations and will stay with me for ever. The visit to the graves was also a moving experience. The evening following the lovely banquet and great entertainment was a fitting tribute to a very special day.

I must say that to meet so many wonderful people who worked so hard to make our time with you so memorable was truly an uplifting experience. Once again on behalf of myself and my mother, Mayo Murphy, formerly Dawson, I would like to thank all concerned for making my trip to Ireland one of the high lights of my travels, one which I will always cherish.

Shauna Murphy.

****

Australian Defence Staff,
Australian High Commission
Australian House, London

1st April 2003.

Dear friends,

Thank you for your kind invitation to attend the upcoming Memorial Service for the Australian airmen at Fermanagh in August this year. I would be very pleased to attend on behalf of the Royal Australian Air Force. If you could please advise me of the details and timing of the ceremony, I will ensure it is placed in my calendar.

I look forward to the occasion and meeting you in August.

Yours,

Tim Owen,

Group Captain, Air Force Advisor.

****

Group Captain M.A. Sharp
Senior Royal Air Force
Officer, Northern Ireland
Royal Air Force
Aldergrove

24th June 2003

Dear Friends

Thank you for your letter dated 24th March 2003 regarding the memorial Service to be held at the View Point, Lough Navar, County Fermanagh on 17th August 2003. I am sorry for the delay in replying, but I have been seeking approval for us to have a helicopter available to participate in a Fly Past at the Service and it has taken a little time to confirm the arrangements. However, I am pleased to confirm that we should be able to provide a Sea King Mk3 from the Search and Rescue Force for the flypast. The aircraft and crew will be from 202 Squadron, which we thought would be the most fitting for the event.

I very much hope to be able to attend the ceremony with my wife and I would be happy to participate in either a formal capacity or as just one of the crowd as you see fit.

Yours sincerely,

Martin A. Sharp.

****

Royal Air Force
Aldergrove

4th September 2003

Dear Friends,

Thank you for your letter of 29th August regarding 202 Squadron's participation in the dedication service at Lough Navar the other week. As I said at the time, we in today's Royal Air Force know that we have a debt to our forbearers and are humbled by the respect and interest by those in the local community towards those who lost their lives in the area in World War 2.

May I say once again how moved I was by the ceremony and time and effort put in by local people to mark the loss of these men. It was a pleasure and an honour to have been invited to participate.

Yours sincerely,

Martin Sharp,
Group Captain.

****

The Returned and Services
League of Australia
ANZAC House, Sydney

15th August 2003

Dear Friends,

I write on behalf of the membership of the New South Wales Branch of the Returned and Services League of Australia to offer our thanks and gratitude to you and others involved.

Jill McInnes brought to our attention the work you are doing in the placement of memorial stones at the crash sites within Fermanagh County, Northern Ireland.

Our membership, some who may have flown from Fermanagh air base, are well aware of how much it means to former comrades and families that their loved ones are not only remembered, but looked after by good people. Thank you for what you have done and you are continuing to do for our Australian servicemen and the many nationalities that are embraced by the soil of Ireland.

Yours sincerely,

Keith N. Hall,
State President.

****

From Bruce Johnston whose brother, F/Sgt. A.S. Johnston, died when Halifax EB134 crashed near Tuam, Co. Galway.

E-mail 8th August 2009. We have arrived home again after a very busy period of sightseeing in Dublin and Paris. Now, there has been a lot of talk with friends about where we have been, what we have seen, what was it all like etc., and I must say that our visit to Ireland ranks very highly in our revelations. First was the warm welcome we received from Anne Tierney and the folks at Tuam, and the kindness you extended to us in the North. Thank you for devoting so much of your time in guiding us to Irvinestown and your thoughtfulness in organising the flowers and arranging for us to meet Breege and Doug Hudson. It was all greatly appreciated.

Best wishes from Bruce.

****

From Maurice and Gladys Duffill, Queensland, Australia.
16th August 2009.

Just a brief note to thank you for your efforts on our behalf. We are now comfortable that we know of the life of Sgt. Ronald Oldfield, my Uncle who died in the crash of Catalina AM 265 on the 21st March 1941. I am sure many are grateful for your dedicated research.

Gladys and Maurice Duffill.

****

From Gary Pentland, Gortin, Co. Tyrone.
23rd June 2008.

Many thanks for your letter of 12th May with the information about F/O M.V. Waring's cousin in New Zealand, Mrs. Dyan Tucker and a copy of her lovely poem " Why Does Nana Cry".

Regarding your comments about what we did. I, my son Ian, and others were involved in the Blue Stacks project from the early 1980's. Jimmy McLaughlin became involved in 1994 with me in the erection of ten other memorials, one as far away as Clare Island in Co. Mayo. Michael Gallagher and his son were involved with me in the Blue Stacks as were Liam Briody, members of his family, Joe McDermott and also Seamus Gormley from Whitehill, Ballinamallard who made the first cut in the rock with his disc cutter on Sunday 7th August 1988. A team of helpers carried an electric generator and other equipment to the crash site. The generator was lent to us by Milligan's Contractor's. The plaque was permanently installed by Harold Walls of Walls engineering and me on Sunday 27th October 1991.

Best wishes from Gary Pentland.

Gary is presently working on a memorial plaque near Killybegs, Co. Donegal., where Sunderland ML743 crashed on 14th March 1945. He set a very high standard and example for others of us to follow and become involved in erecting memorials, as it was not possible for him to do them all.

****

Sunderland landing on Erne

Group Captain J.A. Frizzle, 252, Parklea Drive, Allen Heights, R.R.2 Tantallon, Nova Scotia, Canada. 31st Jan. 1991. Quote, "Also flying control, which included A/C mooring area, were nearly all ex-World War One R.A.F. pilots who knew little about modern aircraft, resulting in frequent disagreements with Squadron Commanders. I was in 422 Squadron (Canadian). We lost I believe 4 aircraft. One was lost basically on a transportation trip on the way to Gibraltar. This one we believed shot down by a German JU88. The second aircraft, Sunderland NJ175 was lost after an engine failed shortly after take-off with a full fuel load. Flying control directed the Captain to proceed to an open ocean area about 20 miles away, jettison the fuel before returning to land. Before reaching the ocean area, the wind milling propeller seized and flew off, destroying another engine on the same side. The aircraft crashed with the resultant loss of three crew members.

I believe the aircraft should have been directed to land immediately at Archdale. I later had occasion to land with a full load with no difficulties. Hospital facilities were in an old Castle several miles from Archdale and it

was rumoured that if you went in with a cold you came out with pneumonia.
Sincerely yours, Joe Frizzle.

****

In an e-mail to his friend Peter Daly, in Ireland, Chuck Singer said "I hope all is well with you Peter. Bob and I are leaving for a trip to Canada on the 21st of this month August 2007. We are going to visit my youngest brother, Harry that I had not seen since he was two years old, until last spring. We lost track of him when we all were sent to foster homes when we were small kids. What a nice guy he is and I am looking forward to our trip. Harry lives in Northern Ontario where it is beautiful.

Take good care of yourself,

Chuck S.

Peter Daly's father was one of the surgeons who attended Chuck in the Sheil Hospital in Ballyshannon after the crash of NJ 175.

****

Harry Singer and his wife Bette

Later, I had an e-mail from Harry Singer and his wife, Bette

Hi Joe; I was sent to a home at the age of 4 when our mother died. When I turned 20, I was informed by the Children's Aid Society that a Mr. John Logan (my mother's brother) was interested in me. (He has long since passed a way.) When I met him he informed me that I had two brothers and a sister, Margaret, Charles, and Bud. I met Margaret and kept in touch with her until her death about 12 years ago. We found out that Bud had died and Chuck lived in the States. I had no idea.

Our daughter Joanne went on her computer and found Chuck living in Green Acres, Florida and found his address. Bette and I winter in Florida so we decided to find him. We found his home but there was no one home so we left a card with our Canadian phone number on it. About a month later we were back in Canada and Charlie phoned us as he was in Canada visiting his brother-in-law. He said he would like to meet us so we told him to come over which he did. We phoned our three kids and they came over to meet him and a few months later, all his family and our family had a reunion in Florida. I think there were 23 of our family alone and his kids, friends and granddaughter. We had a great time and since then Chuck, Bob, and Jackie, came to Canada and stayed 4 days with us, and we visit back and forth in Florida, so we are constantly in touch.

What a wonderful few years for Chuck, coming back to Ireland, getting in touch with his old Squadron and a few former comrades. When I was on a visit to Millville, New Jersey in 2003 Chuck and Bob came all the way to see me. My brother Sean went to Florida on several occasions to visit a cousin of ours and each time Chuck Singer drove him every place he had to go – what a true friend Chuck is!

****

Gail Robertson of Calgary, Alberta, Canada, knew that her Uncle, Delmer Ronald McGilliveray, had been in a plane crash somewhere in Ireland during World War 2. On a trip to Ireland with her daughter, she inquired in the Library in Enniskillen, seeking information. Margaret Kane recommended that she contact me, which she did. We met in her hotel in Bundoran, and there I was able to tell her that her Uncle Ronald had survived the crash of Halifax 120 when it ditched in Mullaghmore Bay, Sligo, on 9th February 1945. Sadly, her uncle was to lose his life when his plane crashed over Germany a short time after. We keep in touch all the time, and Gail and Dana have returned to Ireland for other trips.

****

Mrs. Mary Garston whose brother, Sgt. Elvet Parry, lost his life when Sunderland W4036 crashed in Lough Erne, on the 18th November 1943, came on a visit to Fermanagh, in October 2007. With her sister, Ida Mould, she attended a wreath laying ceremony on Lough Erne, in memory of those who died in the crash. I met with the two ladies, and gave a copy of my Donegal book to Ida, and promised to send a copy to Mary. She wrote a lovely letter of thanks when she got the book. She told me that they were not given any information other than the bare facts, back in 1943, so she had learned so much on the visit to Enniskillen.

"We had always assumed that Elvet was in the rear turret, which must have broken off, hence the recovery of his body. It was comforting to know that he was in the 'Ward Room' with the rest of the crew. So many answers to questions asked over the last 64 years. Your book tells of many such boys – the sad losses – all so young – all terribly grieved over. It is evident that the people of County Fermanagh, especially yourself and Breege, have kept faith with the lost airmen and have brought much comfort to their families. I was in Belleek in August 1968, and had gone to Enniskillen, to see if there was any kind of memorial. Thanks to you, I now know there is one.

****

Ida also wrote on 19th October 2007. Thank you very much for the book, I could see when we were in Enniskillen that it would be most interesting and it is. I will never forget our stay and was sorry not to have been able to see the monument at Loch Navar, but we will return again, and stay a little longer. I was only eleven in 1943, and hardly knew him. It was only at the lake that I really appreciated what we had lost. Not just the young man Elvet was, but the children and grandchildren he should have had for us to love.

****

Sgt. John Bosanka Green also died in the crash of Sunderland W4036. His sister, Mrs. Aine Hine, England, also attended the ceremony on Lough Erne. I gave her a copy of my book, and when she went home, she sent me a lovely letter of thanks and appreciation, "and how you helped to make it a memorable occasion."

Regards from Aine Hine

****

CHAPTER 16

The Ports and Irish Neutrality

The granting of the use of the Donegal Corridor in the early stages of the war, proved to be of much better help to Britain, and the American air craft, than returning the ports to Britain. During 1940, there was a period of time called the 'Phoney War', before action became really serious. America was supplying air craft, and other materials, to Britain under, 'a Lend-Lease basis', and did not enter into the conflict in Europe until after the Japanese bombed Pearl Harbour, when Germany declared war on the U.S.A.

The ports concerned were Berehaven, Cobh, and Cork, on the south coast, Killarry and Galway on the west coast, and Lough Swill on the north coast. Apart from Lough Swilly, which was very close to the Derry port in Northern Ireland, the others were within easy striking distance from German occupied France, with its airfields and U-Boat pens. It is certainly arguable that the provision of the Donegal Corridor made a far more significant contribution to the Battle of the Atlantic, than any possible benefits Britain could have obtained from using the ageing First World War treaty ports. These Ports were largely indefensible from air and U-boat attacks, and their overt use, as opposed to the covert nature of the Donegal Corridor, would have given Hitler an excuse to invade Ireland. Its occupation would clearly have been strategically disastrous for Britain.

There were other ways in which Eire accommodated Britain, for example, during the war, as Shannon and Foynes were the last place to fuel planes for the long flight across the Atlantic, military air craft from various nations refuelled at these two bases. A total of 1,400 aircraft, and 15,000 military personnel, passed through Foynes airport during the war years. Other aircraft that landed at these bases, or other Irish air fields, were refuelled and took off again for their home base. It would be safe to assume that Britain had stores of fuel in Eire for those purposes. The large number of volunteers who went to England, or crossed the border into N. Ireland to join British forces, amounted to 160,000. This figure was arrived at from the official records, as each person joining up had to give the particulars of their next of kin. At least seven Victoria Crosses were awarded to men from Eire during the war, and one from N. Ireland. This service man was not from a part of Belfast noted for supporting the union. Many other awards were gained for outstanding bravery and service. At least 10,000 Irish men died in the service of the Allied forces during World War 2. Another 200,000 people, who were outside the age for joining up, went to work on factories, building air fields, or on many jobs where labour was required. Each person had to obtain a travel permit, and there was a record of the total numbers. Not included in the figures are the number of Irish already working and living in England, or those who served with the commonwealth countries, and in the USA forces. For a neutral country, Ireland's contribution to the Allies in man power alone was considerable.

It is worth noting that neither Germany nor Japan had embassies in Ireland; their interests were served by Legations, as were those of Britain. As Ireland was then a commonwealth nation, Britain did not require an Embassy. The German government had requested that diplomatic relations be upgraded to ambassadorial level, but by the terms of the Irish External Relations Act 1936, any German ambassador would have had to have his credentials addressed to King George V1, and so Mr. de Valera declined the request. The principal reason so many Irish joined the Allied Military forces, and work force, was financial; there was little or no employment in Ireland, and the return of money to the families at home kept them above the poverty line.

What few air craft the Irish had were constantly on patrol along the south and west coast. If they sighted any German planes, ships, or U-boats, they radioed the information back to base, with the knowledge that the British listened to all their radio communications, and so could take any action necessary. The American Ambassador to Ireland, Mr. David Grey, was an enthusiastic wild life shooter, who would go the marshes in County Wexford on shooting trips. On one occasion, he requested that Irish air craft should not fly over the area, as they were disturbing the birds. Mr. Grey was not a career diplomat; he got the post as his wife was a near relation of the U.S. Presidents wife. A popular subject of malicious false propaganda spread about Ireland, was that German U-boats were re-fuelled by Ireland. The country did not have enough fuel for its own needs, and the U-boats used a special diesel that was only obtainable in Germany. The Germans had large tanker U-boats, known as 'Milk Cows', and they could refuel the standard U-boat in mid-Atlantic. Some of them actually went up the St. Lawrence River and torpedoed ships being assembled for convoys.

Ireland had few ships of its own during the war. The government managed to buy one ship in Spain, and three others in America. Government Minister Frank Aiken, was sent to America to attempt to buy some ship, but the Roosevelt government turned him down. Then, by chance, he was introduced to a lady who was of high rank in the American Navy. She was of Irish parentage, and due to her influence, Aiken was able to purchase three vessels. As Ireland was neutral, Irish ships continued to sail with full navigation lights. They had large tricolours, and the word "Eire" painted in large letters on their sides and decks. At that time, Allied ships travelled in convoy for protection from the U-boat 'wolf packs'. If a ship was torpedoed, it was left behind, since the other ships could not stop for fear of becoming a target. Irish ships that were in the convoys always stopped. They rescued almost 700 British merchant seamen from the Atlantic. In some cases they rescued air men, whose planes had to ditch in the ocean. However, several Irish ships were attacked by belligerents on both sides. Over 20% of Irish sailors on clearly marked neutral vessels lost their lives. On one occasion, when Ireland was in dire need of wheat supplies, the Government applied to England for wheat. The application was turned down in no uncertain terms, and they were informed that being neutral, they were not entitled to any wheat. Ireland then said, then in that case, they would no longer export any Guinness to Britain. This would have been a disaster for the British work force. Ireland got its wheat – the English got their Guinness!!

To understand the effect the false propaganda had on the average English person, it is necessary to illustrate their feeling towards their neighbours. The following is a letter that was published in the well-known magazine "The Ireland's Own", in 1991. The letter had regard to an article published in the magazine, entitled "**de Valera's reply to Churchill**".

"**I read with interest the article in a recent Ireland's Own, on Mr. de Valera's reply to Mr. Churchill in 1945, on the issue of Irish neutrality. I believe that Mr. Churchill would have more easily found in his heart the** generosity 'to acknowledge that there is a small nation that stood alone not for one year or two.......against aggression' had Mr. de Valera found in his heart the generosity to offer any help he could to his old enemy in her hour of desperate need, when as he admits, she stood alone.

Had Mr. de Valera done this, had he not allowed rancour over old wrongs to blind him to the very real evil which Britain faced, and which might so easily have prevailed, he would have done great honour to his country's name.

However he chose a smug neutrality, with possibly a degree of Schadenfreude. He allowed his country to become a safe haven for spies, and worse, he denied to allied shipping the use of the ports of the west of Ireland, which meant that exhausted convoys had much further to travel in dangerous waters, and which undoubtedly led to the deaths of many seamen.

Did Mr. deValera really imagine that if Britain were invaded, Hitler would have respected his neutrality, except at the price of the soul of his people? Undoubtedly, had he toe'd the German line in every way that Hitler demanded, he could have lived in peace. Would he have been prepared to do that, and to happily shake hands with members of a government which was enslaving Poles and denying Jews the most basic human rights, even before the 'Final Solution' was brought into play? Did Mr. de Valera really not see that the issues at stake in the war went well beyond any quarrels he still had with the government of Britain?

Ireland's neutrality, in one of the very few just wars in history, was a matter of shame for my Irish mother, whose English husband was fighting, and is a matter of shame and anger for me. Mr. de Valera was a great leader in many ways, but how much greater he could have been had he taken the opportunity for true generosity in 1939.

****

The letter was signed by the young lady, giving her address, so I thought that as a person who had a considerable amount of knowledge of the true facts of Ireland's neutrality, that I should write to her and acquaint her of them.

In my letter to the young lady I pointed out that the views promoted on the subject of neutrality are of a much maligned nature, based on opinions, which in many aspects are contrary to the actual facts. I grew up in a border village during the war, and therefore was witness to some of the matters I wish to enlighten you on. War time maps were in colour, with Britain and its colonies, including Northern Ireland, shown in pink or red. Neutral countries, of which there were few, were coloured in yellow. Was there any significance in this? If all the propaganda about the Irish was to be believed perhaps there should have been a little white feather on the map of Ireland!

Eamon de Valera, the Taoiseach, (Prime Minister), had the full support of his people, and of all the opposition political parties. Should he and his government have decided to abolish their stance of neutrality, the next logical step would have been to declare war on Germany. What the Irish would have used for weapons we can only surmise. In its neutral state, Ireland did not escape the terrors of the German Luftwaffe. The county of Wexford, and a number of other towns in the midlands were bombed, as was Dublin city. Belfast, which was in the war zone, suffered terribly as a result of German air raids. When the fires were raging in Belfast, one of the leading Unionist politicians, who would not have been a bosom friend of the Taoiseach, sanctioned a phone call directly to de Valera seeking assistance. The result was that all available fire appliances from Dublin city, county, and other towns on the east coast, were dispatched immediately to Belfast.

I pointed out that the fallacy that Ireland was a haven for German spies was completely erroneous. I suggested that she read a book, "Spies in Ireland", written by a German, Enno Stephan, published by The New English Library Ltd., a Four Square Book. It was first published in the German language as 'Geheimauftrag Irland'. Another book I referred to was 'Hitler's Irish Voices', by David O'Donoghue. Both books show that the shelf lives of German spies in Ireland averaged about three days, from arrival to capture and internment. I also told her about the Donegal Corridor, and several of the many other ways that Ireland had accommodated the allied forces. I expressed the hope that, when the real facts are taken into account, de Valera may get some belated credit for the support that he gave to the Allied cause during World War 2. The actions of de Valera and the Irish people would indicate that neutrality was not what it appeared to be, nor was it, as some would like to portray it, as having been. I hope that the facts that I have presented will in some small way soothe the shame and anger that you and your mother feel for the land of her birth.

I have chosen to write direct to you rather than conduct a discussion through the medium of a journal. This is not an attempt to change any strong views you might have on de Valera; it is only to make you aware of the positive things that he did, and approved of.

Yours sincerely, Joe O'Loughlin.

****

Early in June I had a very gracious reply to my letter.

Dear Mr. O'Loughlin,

Thank you very much indeed for your interesting letter which has just reached me. I am glad that you wrote to me personally as had you written to the pages of 'Ireland's Own' I should not have known, as I do not get it where I am now.

You made some very good and well-reasoned points in your letter and you seem to have a very fair view. From what you say I probably was rather unfair to Mr. de Valera. Certainly I recognise that Irish people fought very bravely, not only in World War 2 but in other conflicts. In fact, reading the history of the British Empire makes one realise how big a part Irish solders played in many major events in its history. Never for a moment would I want to deny the bravery of Irish servicemen and women. Also, I would never have believed that the average Irish man and woman in the street would have wanted an Axis victory.

I had never considered the possibility of a German invasion of Ireland had she not remained neutral, unless Britain had been invaded first, but obviously that would have been a possibility. I had not realised, either, the help the Government gave to Belfast after the bombing; most interesting. In fact so much of what you told me was of great interest, and someday I hope to read some of the books you recommended. You clearly have a great grasp of history, and your letter was a pleasure to read. Thank you also for the map and brochure which I also found interesting.

Again, many thanks for your letter.

Yours sincerely, S.H.

****

Another story about the part played by an Irishman who risked his life to help Allied airmen during WW2, is that of Monsignor Hugh O'Flaherty, from Co. Kerry in the Irish Free State. He was a diplomat attached to the Vatican in Rome. The Monsignor put his life on the line on numerous occasions during the years when Germany occupied Italy. He set up an escape system to assist allied military personnel who had escaped from P.O.W. camps, or had otherwise found themselves behind enemy lines. He gave them refuge in safe places while he organised false documents, and provided then with civilian clothing. As a result of his clandestine operations, a large number of both British and American personnel were repatriated and re-joined their units.

A couple of amusing stories about German spies in Ireland. One had come ashore in Co. Kerry, from a U-boat, was walking along a road that ran parallel to a railway line. He met with a local man and asked him in very polite English, "My good man can you tell me when the next train will be going to Dublin?" The Kerry man replied, "I really cannot say, as the last train to run on this line was 15 years ago, and I have no idea when there will be another one".

A young Irish man was working in Germany, and the authorities decided to send him to Ireland as a spy. He was parachuted from a plane and made his way to the home of his father, who was a Garda sergeant in Co. Mayo. There was a reward of £100 for the capture of any German spy. The father immediately arrested his son who was interned in the Curragh, and collected the reward. When the war was over, and the lad released, the father gave him the £100 and told him to go and do something useful with his life.

When the Lough Erne based flying boat came down in Bundoran Bay, one of the crew was left on board as a guard. The Irish army sent one of their soldiers to the plane on guard duty. The two men were not happy about the situation and were not enjoying each other's company. Eventually, they started to chat and discovered that they were both from Tipperary. The Irish lad considered this was a cause for celebration, so he took the little boat tied up to the plane, went into Bundoran and got a liberal supply of Guinness. Needless to say they had an enjoyable spell of duty.

CHAPTER 17

The Daughter of a Donegal Emigrant

Padrig Pearce Molloy, with his parents left their native Meenagolan, Ardara, Co. Donegal home, and settled in Canada, in 1926. His daughter, Kathleen Claire Winters, became a noted aviator, author and speaker.
On 19th September 2008 I received an e-mail from Kathleen C. Winters.

I enjoyed perusing your web site, which came to my attention via a Google Alert on "naval aviation," one of several writing projects now consuming my time. For many reasons, your book "Voices of the Donegal Corridor", interested me. I'm an aviation writer, and the daughter of an Irishman still living in Canada, and born in 1918, in Meenagolan, County Donegal. Please let me know if this book is available for purchase in the United States.
Bless you for your work as a historian, vital work necessary, but so often a thankless job.

Kindest regards,

Kathleen C. Winters, Author of "Anne Morrow Lindberg; First lady of the Air".

****

I replied to Kathleen's mail, and told her that it might be a problem getting the book in the U.S., but if she would send me her home address, I would send her a copy. Rather than send payment through the usual system, I suggested that we use the old Irish barter method, and in exchange she send me a copy of her "Anne Morrow Lindberg" book. When sending me her home address, in St. Paul Park, Minnesota, she said an exchange would be great. She told me that her father, with his parents, came to Canada in 1926. He was aged 8. Now suffering from dementia, he sometimes talks of Ireland. She had never visited Donegal, or Ireland, but said it was high on her list of priorities. She told me that she was working on a biography of Amelia Earhart, who landed in Derry after a trans-Atlantic flight, and that she would be pleased if I could give her any help with the story.

Our correspondence developed, and I sent her a number of books on Donegal and Ireland. As a result, she became very interested in the history of her father's homeland. She told me that she was not only a fixed wing pilot, but also a glider pilot. Kathleen also told me, that she was part Native American, as her mother was from the Chippewa tribe in Ontario. We exchanged many books. I sent her books of Irish interest, and she, in return, sent me books with the history of America. We also exchanged the traditional music of both countries. An Irish born friend of her Dad's was reading the Donegal Corridor book for him. "The correspondence, and the books, have brought me closer to my Irish roots", she said and "I can't thank you enough. Little by little I am starting to understand my ancestors and I knew nothing about Donegal before this".

12th August 2010

Dear Joe,

I was thrilled to get the 'Flying in Ireland' magazine yesterday, which I instantly devoured. Actually, I didn't eat it, but you know what I mean. Always of interest to me, is news of international events and airlines, in addition to Ireland itself, and its aircraft and clubs. Then as a bonus, I found an article about the R34 flights on the back page, which I had written about in my Earhart book.

Best wishes from Kathleen.

****

Sadly, this was to be the last message I got from my friend Kathleen Claire Winters, nee Molloy. Just one week later, she died from a brain haemorrhage, on the 19th August 2010. On the 22nd of August, I had an e-mail from her husband, Jim, to tell me that she had passed away after a short illness. She never lived to see her book on Amelia Earhart published. Monday, the 21st May 2012, was the 80th anniversary of Amelia's flight across the Atlantic, the first woman to do so. She had set off from Newfoundland for Paris, in her Lockheed Vega plane. But landing, instead, in Derry, Ireland, she asked a lady in the field she landed on "Where am I?" The lady said you are in Gallagher's pasture. The epic flight got full coverage in the papers, radio, and television, in 2012, and a film was discovered, with much footage, on Amelia's time in Derry. Sadly, Amelia Earhart was lost with her navigator in 1937, on a trans-Pacific flight.

The book on Amelia Earhart, titled "The Turbulent Life of an American Icon", was published in November 2010, and I obtained a copy from Amazon. Due to a worldwide interest in the Donegal Corridor, I had gained a wonderful friend, whose roots were in Donegal.

More than a place to begin or end a journey, Donegal gives the heart a place to call home

THE DEPARTURE BAY

I was in the place of departure,
I know not the time of my flight,
I hope its way off in the future,
But it could be I'm flying tonight.

The flight I await goes to Heaven,
I know that it's lovely up there,
For I've read their fine brochure, the Bible,
And I speak to them oft in my prayer.

It costs very little to go there,
You take nothing with you at all,
And you pay by the way you behave every day,
And you wait for St. Peter to call.

As I wait for the start of my journey,
There's so many things I can see,
Like someone in need of a word or a deed,
So I do what's expected of me.

So I wait at the place of departure,
Never too sure when to fly,
But I hope that when I die,
There's a chance I'll meet you,
We can all pay the fare if we try.

CONCLUSION

To produce a work such as this is a major undertaking. So many documents have to be checked, and keyed in. While newspaper reports in recent events are readily available, they are practically non-existent about events during the World War 2 years, in the Irish Free State, or "Eire", as it became known as. Very strict censorship was imposed on all newspapers, but thankfully, the Military Archives in Dublin became available in the late 1990's. The reader will understand, I hope; that there will be errors in this work, mainly of a minor type.

One of the primary objects in writing this book, is to pay tribute to the over 350 young men who died while serving on Lough Erne, and also remember their comrades who survived.

Another object is to make known the real facts of the neutrality of Eire; many people were brain washed into believing the false malicious propaganda spread by those who objected to the Irish stance of neutrality. Generally, people are amazed, and pleased, to learn the real facts. One contact was surprised to learn that Eire even had an army!

Families who lost loved ones in accidents, or whose planes 'Failed to Return' from missions, had little or no information as to what had happened. Having read my book, and found my website, many of them contacted me, and I was able, in most cases, to give them the crash history they required. This was a great consolation, and brought a sense of closure to the families after over 60 years of not knowing.

Their words of appreciation and their friendship has been my reward for helping them. This work would not have been possible without the help and guidance of a number of World War 2 aviation historians, here in Ireland; for this I am extremely grateful. I have an advantage in the fact that I actually lived through this period of our history. As I live in the area, and grew up here during the war years, most of the facts recorded here are connected either directly or indirectly to the Lough Erne bases of Castle Archdale, Killadeas and St. Angelo. While the projects carried out by Breege McCusker, a few willing helpers, and myself, were done on 'a shoe string' financially, we are extremely grateful to Paddy Crowther of the N. Ireland Air Crews Association, who made generous contributions for several of our projects. Apart from the incidents here in Co. Fermanagh, no similar work has been done on the hundreds of crashes that happened in Northern Ireland. That is a task for another author on another day.